# WE ARE PRODUCTS

**Dr Biju P.R.** is assistant professor at the Department of Political Science, Government Brennen College, Thalassery, Kerala. He is a writer, teacher and researcher who tracks the trinity of everyday technology, society and social change. He keeps himself engaged with topics on artificial intelligence, love, sexuality, relationships, discrediting fake news, the effects of Internet pornography, and the link between technology and society in India. He is also the author of *Political Internet* (2016), *Intimate Speakers* (2017), *Selfie Sex* (2018) and *Slave Technology* (2019). He is currently working on the history of the social evolution of technology from hominids to humanoids, which argues that machines are capable of replacing not only human muscles, but brain functions.

'We are social robots, reduced to data. In this accessible study of the contemporary social media, Biju P.R. argues that we're subjected to a new, extractive force: digital colonialism. Unless we raise awareness about the ways machine learning, algorithms and artificial intelligence are manipulating our everyday lives, this new form of digital imperialism will remain uncontested.'

—**Geert Lovink**
Media theorist, internet critic and founder of
Institute of Network Cultures (INC)

# WE ARE PRODUCTS
## HOW AI INVADES OUR LIFE

# BIJU P.R.

RUPA

Published by
Rupa Publications India Pvt. Ltd 2023
7/16, Ansari Road, Daryaganj
New Delhi 110002

*Sales Centres:*
Allahabad Bengaluru Chennai
Hyderabad Jaipur Kathmandu
Kolkata Mumbai

Copyright © Biju P.R. 2023

The views and opinions expressed in this book are the author's own and the facts are as reported by him which have been verified to the extent possible, and the publishers are not in any way liable for the same.

All rights reserved.
No part of this publication may be reproduced, transmitted, or stored in a retrieval system, in any form or by any means, electronic, mechanical, photocopying, recording or otherwise, without the prior permission of the publisher.

P-ISBN: 978-93-5702-064-0
E-ISBN: 978-93-5702-061-9

First impression 2023

10 9 8 7 6 5 4 3 2 1

The moral right of the author has been asserted.

Printed in India

This book is sold subject to the condition that it shall not, by way of trade or otherwise, be lent, resold, hired out, or otherwise circulated, without the publisher's prior consent, in any form of binding or cover other than that in which it is published.

*For Dr Gayathri O,*
*She is hundred per cent forgiving!*

# Contents

*Foreword* ix

*Introduction* xi

1. Self-Inventing Machines 1
2. Cognitive Disaster 14
3. Intelligent Machines Will Conquer Us 26
4. Attention for Sale 36
5. Data: Instrument of Capitalism? 47
6. Information Cocoons and Echo Chambers 55
7. Mind Accessed by Data Firms 62
8. Robots: Our Non-Human Friends 68
9. Data Is the Chauffeur 76
10. Data-Controlled Deliveries 85
11. Internet in Our Bodies? 90
12. Custom-Generated Thoughts 100
13. Information Cartels 106
14. Our 'Datafied' Life 113
15. America Everywhere 119
16. Data at Risk 129

| | |
|---|---:|
| 17. We Have Something to Hide | 136 |
| 18. Our Lives as Marionettes | 144 |
| 19. Social Contract: Violated? | 154 |
| 20. We Are Data | 160 |
| *Endnotes* | 171 |
| *Acknowledgements* | 189 |

# Foreword

This is an interesting and informative book. As we try and make sense of the disruptions to our settled social life by the advances of technology, especially those brought about by the innovations in artificial intelligence, this book, *We Are Products,* is a good companion in this endeavour. Dr Biju P.R. has, through 20 slim chapters, presented us with a checklist of issues that we must think about as we probe further these transformations. He has placed his book within ongoing debates taking place in both the academic and policy world on the impacts of these new algorithm-driven technologies, and has offered the reader, in an accessible format—where he uses the brief life stories and social contexts within which ordinary persons are located, from shopping to romance, to foreground these issues of technology converting us from consumers to products. For example, the chapter 'Cognitive Disaster' begins with a discussion on emotions and how these get manipulated by the new technologies. Similarly, the chapter 'Attention for Sale' connects with the arguments of scholars who make similar points, such as Shoshana Zuboff, who sees in these new technologies the emergence and growth of surveillance systems. Engineers and technologists respond to these advances in digital technology by identifying the technical problems and attempting to solve them. Social scientists, in contrast, respond by examining their impact on human societies, especially on human interactions. As a political scientist, Dr Biju's narrative is one of awe in the power of technology and a lamentation over its disruptive, even destructive, impacts. It is a timely book, since, in India, these are questions that need to be debated. His treatment should be regarded as the first take on the issues of disruptive digital technologies. It is a good basis for us to begin this critical conversation.

**Peter Ronald deSouza**, former director,
Indian Institute of Advanced Study, Shimla, and
D.D. Kosambi Visiting Professor at Goa University

# Introduction

When Google was founded in 1998 by Larry Page and Sergey Brin, it was just a search engine. Now, its portfolio has transformed itself into Alphabet, encompassing several futuristic industries: anti-ageing, artificial intelligence (AI), surgical robots, contact lenses, self-driving technology, wind energy using kites and drone delivery. Alphabet even runs a semi-secret research facility called X.[1]

But this tech story is not confined only to Google. When founded by Jeff Bezos in 1994, Amazon was just an online marketplace for books. Now, it has expanded to e-readers, online grocery shopping, fresh-food marketing, digital music, movies, gaming and many others. Amazon Prime Air is an unmanned drone delivery system. Amazon Go is a physical shopping service operated with automated technology, with no queues and a self-checkout option.

Similarly, leading tech giants, such as Apple, Facebook, Uber and others have invested in futuristic technology. So has Elon Musk, the billionaire tech entrepreneur who is the co-founder of PayPal; CEO of SpaceX and, now, Twitter; and CEO and product architect of Tesla Motors. Musk has had some crazy ideas: satellite-based Internet connectivity; hyperloop (a technology currently in the development stage that plans to transport people in individual aluminium pods through specially constructed low-pressure tubes); affordable space travel; and establishing a colony on Mars. These sound like crazy ideas but can be made possible only if humans work alongside technology.

Tech firms dealing with such ground-breaking ideas are expanding. These firms block the growth of other start-up ideas that have the potential to be future rivals through mergers. Examples include the acquisition of Whole Foods Market and Zappos by Amazon; WhatsApp and Instagram by Meta (Facebook); and mapping service Waze, smart home products Nest and ad company DoubleClick by Google.

The business model that tech giants follow is complicated. The largest retail stores like Alibaba or Flipkart neither manufacture nor create a product. The largest book-selling stores like Amazon don't produce their own books. The world's largest online cab aggregator, Uber, does not own any cars. Hotel networks like Yatra (yatra.com) do not own a hotel. One of the largest social networking sites in the world, Facebook, has multi-year deals with news media companies and video creators, but it does not produce any original content.[2] Social media platforms are so-called because these platforms create a vast pool of users rather than the content we see on them.

The technology that we will see in the future will transform the way we live, think and work. More importantly, our cognitive power, emotions and comprehension skills are likely to be affected. All this will be possible thanks to some crazy, futuristic tech ideas: AI, machine learning, natural language processing, speech recognition, drone delivery system, driverless cars, social robotics and various others.

But these ideas are not just our future—they are our present as well. We are already seeing social robotics replacing parental care, drones delivering grocery orders to our doorstep, software recognizing our natural voice, algorithms identifying images, humanoids replacing sexual partners, machine learning processing applicants' CVs, big data and smart cities enabling autonomous cars, AI placing a house call for a doctor during an emergency, and various other similar purposes. Machines keep getting better and better every day. But we don't know whether they will overtake us at everything. And if so, what then?

English psychologist Charles Spearman, based on a study conducted by French psychologists Alfred Binet and Théodore Simon for the French government, proposed the theory that there must be a single underlying construct for human intelligence. On the other hand, psychologists Robert Sternberg and Howard Gardner championed the idea of specific types of intelligences, such as linguistic, musical, intrapersonal, logical-mathematical, etc. rather than a single overall intelligence. Furthermore, researchers Katja Grace, John Salvatier, Allan Dafoe, Baobao Zhang and Owain Evans, in a paper titled 'Viewpoint: When Will AI Exceed Human Performance? Evidence from AI Experts', predicted that AI will outperform humans in many activities in the next 10 years. Translating languages (by 2024), working in retail (by 2031), driving a truck (by 2027), writing high-school essays (by 2026), writing a bestselling book (by 2049) and performing surgeries (by 2053) are examples of machines outperforming human intelligence in specific fields in the future.[3]

Then there are those who believe that intelligence is unique to humans and that there is a mystery behind our cognitive abilities.[4] Philosophers Colin McGinn and Jerry Fodor, and celebrated psychologist Steven Pinker have been sympathetic to this proposition. We can understand it by looking at a simple example: when a baby cries, it cries for several reasons. Sometimes, it is easy to work out what they want, but it isn't easy to do so on all occasions. There may be times when the baby tends to cry a lot and cannot be comforted. Sometimes, a baby cries for nothing. The reason why a baby cries is a subjective understanding, which is unique to human intelligence. If you design a babysitter algorithm, it's a machine that functions on training data given to its algorithm. You can give inputs about common scenarios of a baby crying. The machine may be given instructional inputs to recognize what causes the baby to cry—hunger, a wet nappy, tiredness, wanting a cuddle, the wind, being too hot or too cold, boredom or overstimulation. How far can a robot recognize subjective scenarios of a baby crying? This makes the mystery behind human intelligence. We cannot discover it. This group claims that machines can never get as smart as humans because there is something magical about intelligence. Creativity is one of the defining features of human beings and can only exist in a human context.

Such contradictory purviews can be perplexing. Is there any reason to claim that creativity belongs to humans alone? Today, machines already show glimpses of creativity in art, sport, medicine and other territories we believed only humans had mastery over. Apple's Siri, Amazon's Alexa and Google Assistant are all voice-controlled personal assistants. Speech recognition devices have now begun undertaking an important human-only activity: speech. Speech recognition technology converts language into text and is deployed across a variety of social situations. Speech is an important human ability to process and interpret the external world, but it is also culturally and socially rooted—embedded in subjective situations, which works better only in human social relationships. Once speech is automated with AI algorithms, it will remove all the subjective roots of speech in human life. Image recognition refers to the technology that identify places, logos, people, objects, buildings and several other variables through images. Google Lens, Amazon's Flow and Screenshop are examples of image recognition technology. With these inventions, it gives way for machines to function similarly to the human ability of recognizing objects, places, people, writings and actions. For example, a 2015 Dutch study showed that the computer diagnosis of prostate cancer using magnetic resonance imaging (MRI) was as accurate as that of human radiologists.[5] A 2016 Stanford study showed that AI can diagnose lung cancer using microscope images even better than human pathologists.[6] We cannot find easy answers, but things are now a bit uncertain and even dangerous as we look forward.

The unbridled commercial use of technology is leading to the destruction of vital human abilities. Our skills are being disrupted by intelligent machines, reducing our lives to computational values. Our value is calculated based on the user data we generate, and data becomes central to our life. These machines are so created that with the data we give them, they can invent and learn things by themselves. They are machines with human-level intelligence that behave like humans in analogous situations.

Our refrigerators, cars, wristwatches, air conditioners, costumes, etc. will get even more Internet-reliant and intelligent in the days to come. Almost all everyday objects will become Internet-enabled. Then there is also the scenario where there will be intercommunication between objects, such as cars and traffic signals, refrigerators and grocery shops, and tech-enabled clothing and surveillance cameras.

This technological sophistication also raises a serious question about our survival. Are we going to be the last generation? The responses are starkly bifurcated between two lines of thought—those who believe in the power of intelligent machines to figure out more opportunities in the future and those predicting doomsday scenarios.

In 2016, uncertainty over AI was spreading across Europe and the United States (US). Google's search engine was making racist auto-complete suggestions. Twitter bots were spreading fake news. Stephen Hawking was worried about AI because machines with intelligence, according to him, would function on their own and learn how to solve problems through self-learning abilities—that too without human intervention, leaving no scope for many activities unique to humans. Far-Right groups were living in algorithm-driven filter bubbles. Facebook was measuring users' personalities to target voters. A Tesla car operating in driverless mode crashed into a truck killing the driver.

The stories of the dangers of AI continue to accumulate. When statistical models got both Brexit and Trump wrong, AI-enabled predictions were called into question. The arbitrary decisions that algorithms are making about us are based on wrong assumptions. While our private lives are becoming increasingly open on the Internet—as we effortlessly share online details of our lifestyle, inner aspirations, movements and social lives—data companies that analyse our data are protected from scrutiny.

According to tech giants such as Microsoft, Google, Apple and Facebook, the most unreliable component in any situation is the human factor. In the past, we thought there were functions that machines could not perform, but now there are functions that humans cannot achieve without help from machines. The most inefficient factor in any situation is humans. So, we can be removed from the equation. The tech world can then assemble new, smart and super intelligent humanoids in our place.

But the real danger is not in machines becoming human-like but humans turning into machines. We have already become more like machines, and our behaviour is predicted and controlled by learning machines piloted by data giants. We become more programmed and robot-like as we embrace more technologies. The line between the emotional and cognitive aspects of humans and the efficiency of intelligent machines will be blurred. Emotions will be lost to efficiency. Cognitive abilities will be lost to machine intelligence.

A society invaded by intelligent machines creates an attention economy. Our attention is a direct input to the capitalist system of production. Every tech giant tries to grab more of our attention to their products through our user data. We use Google so often not simply as a product or for its services but more as a way of life—a tool and a machine that has an impact in almost all areas of our life. The next time you need to make a travel decision, you search Google for the best route and best fare rate offered by a travel agency and transport operator. When you make purchase decisions, choose books to read, movies to watch, dresses to wear—our decisions and connections with tech companies get more intimate. We are completely dependent on tech companies for nearly everything. This way, most of the things that we do in our everyday life are accessible to tech giants. They call this user data, which, among other things, include our phone number and call logs, location status, stored videos and photos, emails and messages we send and receive, browser type, device type, operating system, search items, videos watched, people we communicate and share content with, and the newspapers and media we subscribe to.

Along with providing services to us, tech giants collect our user data to personalize their advertisements and content. They also share our user data with third parties on request. It is their business model. At present, the user data they collect is not based on religion, sexual orientation, health, race or gender explicitly. They are more likely to collect these social stratification data about us in the future. The collection of user data is presently illegal, as most countries do not permit its unauthorized tracking.

Data is the fuel of this economy. These data-hungry corporates are dragging the rest of us towards data colonialism, which is clearly an extension of colonialism in the era of capitalism entering its advanced stage. We are just products! We are just computational values.

In 20 chapters, this book will try to explain how AI, the attention economy and intelligent machines will conquer us. The book tries to sensitize readers to a growing human concern: are we the last generation in the age of AI?

# 1

# Self-Inventing Machines

The other day, I was talking to my student Anitha, who had a volatile family. Her mother had died while giving birth to her brother. Anitha was five when her widowed father remarried, and her stepmother began a relentless course of terror against her. She would pull Anitha by the hair and slap her face. There was never any respite from violence at home for Anitha. Her stepmother's main weapon was emotional abuse—she had an inexhaustible supply of hatred. She had even alleged that their family was getting ruined because of Anitha. Love was only a word in the dictionary for Anitha. Her father was a drunkard who would become verbally abusive when intoxicated and say hurtful things, such as how much it cost to provide clothes and food for Anitha.

Anitha always wished to have someone who could love her like a mother. Perhaps this was a natural human longing for love in times of distress. In the meantime, she fell in love with a distant relative who was her age. Anitha told me, 'I needed someone who would hold my hand when I felt so down.' Her boyfriend would do just that whenever she required it. He could anticipate when she needed a hold to heal her. There was an indefinable emotional connection between them. Anitha continued, 'We used to sit together when there was nobody at his home. We had enough opportunities, but nothing happened—no sex or even any of the other minor stuff.'

As Anitha continued speaking to me, I wondered whether machines could replace this type of emotional connection between humans. A woman wants somebody to hold her hand, and a man consequently understands that the woman wants to be shown love through a touch on the hand. This is a peculiar human quality—the cognitive ability that makes us humans and humane!

I can tell you my story for more clarity. The other day, as I started scrolling down my Facebook timeline, an author and novelist based out of Hyderabad shared a link to a news article on his timeline. The text of the article available on the News18 website was about the response of The Hindu Publishing Group chairman, N. Ram, who had written extensively on the controversial Rafale deal. I went back to my timeline once I had finished reading. Then, I saw a link to an article shared by a Trivandrum-based feminist historian. Current minister of state in the Ministry of Road Transport and Highways and former Indian Army Chief V.K. Singh had made some comment about the student leaders of Jawaharlal Nehru University Shehla Rashid and Kanhaiya Kumar, and he had compared their dissent towards India with those in Israel. The content was available on the web-based platform *Outlook*. Afterwards, as I closed the link and went back to my timeline, something strange happened on my Facebook page. The predictive algorithm on Facebook learnt that, for the time being, I was interested in news related to the Rafale deal and V.K. Singh's comment on student leaders in India. Facebook quickly filtered my timeline and flooded it with just news-related posts. I could now only see news links shared by my Facebook friends as I scrolled down.

Don't you think machines are going to rewire us? I have more than 2,000 friends on Facebook, but I was only seeing links to news shared by many of them. Does it mean that my friends on Facebook are news-obsessed? No! They engage in many activities:

photo uploads, comments, link-sharing to entertaining things and others. But predictive algorithms seemed to try to gain access to my mind and deliver the content they thought I wanted. However, I am not really interested in such content, and I accidentally clicked on the links. But the predictive algorithm was trying to deliver to my taste—according to their calculations!

Facebook uses an algorithm to decide which updates are relevant to you.[7] The friend suggestion that comes to you is in line with the prediction by the algorithm. It makes an assumption from its database—which contains a massive volume of unstructured data about all your activities and then finds some relevant profiles. Moreover, its machine learning algorithm also warns you not to send friend requests to some profiles. According to the inputs given, these profiles do not match your interests. It bans you from sending friend requests after a specified number. The data stored in its algorithm doesn't allow contacting profiles that are not connected to your friends. There may not even be any mutual friends according to the algorithm it has developed. So, your contacts are also controlled by machine learning!

Twitter uses machine learning and deep learning on its feed;[8] it crops photos to show the most exciting parts that you may like according to its algorithm. Machine learning on Twitter learns how much you value that place by analysing factors like time spent and your engagement level. So, the algorithm learns whether you consider it a place where you get all you want. AI assumes that if you haven't been on Twitter for a while, you have probably missed the things that otherwise get you there.[9] The Twitter algorithm, taking advantage of machine learning, predicts what interests you from its data inventory, which stores all of your past activities. So, when you come back to Twitter, you will see content that is relevant to you and pique your interest, as it is tailored to you. The updates on your timeline are not ranked in chronological order.

Instead, it is listed based on a thinking machine, which considers what is relevant for you over a particular period. That means Twitter delivers content that matters to you as fast as possible and in a meaningful way. It uses a machine learning algorithm to predict the relevance on your timeline. Your Twitter feed gets better and better for you by applying machine learning. It allows you to deeply personalize the Twitter experience.

For example, let us consider the Kisan Long March. The All India Kisan Sabha, the peasant's front of the Communist Party of India (Marxist), organized a protest march by the farmers in the state of Maharashtra. Around 40,000–50,000 farmers marched a distance of 180 kilometres from Nashik to Mumbai to gherao the Maharashtra Vidhan Sabha. The march took a few days to reach its destination. You heard the protest, you looked out of the window and you saw all these protesters. Then you went to Twitter and searched for news related to it. Machine learning on Twitter works for you in such instances. It has access to your mind, because it conducts analytics of your past Twitter behaviour. It learns from past activities if a particular individual falls left on the ideological spectrum. On Twitter, you follow all the Left-leaning people and organizations. It knows that you are pro-agriculture. You frequently share Kisan news. It understands you are a civil rights activist, because you frequently tweet about human rights issues. Since you read and share news that you are interested in, Twitter knows you are news-savvy. Now, you find your feed full of people tweeting about the commencement of the protest. It is not because people are relentlessly tweeting about things that are of interest to you but that the machine learning algorithm on Twitter learns your interests and curates the content according to its prediction about what you would like. Twitter will quickly notify you even if you weren't on Twitter at the particular moment when the protest started, letting you know that it was coming your way. Even if the news and other content about the Kisan Long March happened a few days ago and Twitter already reported it, because of the algorithm, you will receive all the information on your feed even if you are late to log in. Now, you can imagine why it is important for you that Twitter delivers you the news for any topic you care about.

Machines with intelligence have gained access to our cognitive mind, and they predict how we behave even before the actual action. Technologies have become monsters because they are so designed to perpetuate themselves. So far, humans have designed technologies that have helped us in areas where we cannot perform within our own physical capacity. The mainstay of all the technologies so far was to buttress human labour. The real brain behind any technology was human. We have been able to control the technologies we created.

Now, there is a great shift in the way we design technologies. The technologies of the future are self-made. When we need a particular technology, the machines learn it themselves and self-design it according to our requirements. That is exactly what we see when predictive algorithms filter news on Facebook and Twitter. Algorithms learn what you need. It is not the human factor that intervenes in delivering you news or other things and provides it to you accordingly; rather, technology predicts and tries to cater to your taste and assist you in every way it can.

The futuristic technologies are not meant to underpin physical labour. They rather cater to our cognitive abilities—our inner mind, the mind that designs everything. If that mind, which designs everything, is designed by technology, we are set to see the death of the human factor in the future, and humans eventually becoming machine-like.

Two important cognitive abilities already being invaded by technology are voice and image recognition software, which are just the tip of the intelligence iceberg that awaits us. One example of voice recognition is the virtual assistant, which has software that can recognize and respond to voice commands. The four dominant ones today are Amazon's Alexa, Apple's Siri, Google's Assistant and Microsoft's Cortana. Facebook is also said to be releasing their version. You can request all sorts of information by interacting with a virtual assistant. Weather forecast, movie reviews, your favourite radio station, news, recipes and sports updates. You can tell them to remember your shopping list or to set the alarm. If your devices are connected to the Internet, you can control them through the virtual assistant as well, such as your electric lights, electric kettle, air conditioner, refrigerator, television and others.

Image recognition technology is not in the future but already part of our present. Data companies such as Tesla, Facebook, Google, Uber, Apple and Adobe Systems heavily use this technology.[10] Image recognition software can do everything that a human visual system can do. TensorFlow by Google, DeepFace by Facebook and Project Oxford by Microsoft are great examples of deep learning image recognition systems.

If we check the spam folder in our email account, majority of those emails will not be not relevant to us. Who decided that we don't need to see all those spam emails? The answer is machine learning. We usually go to Amazon to shop for watches and shoes, or to Netflix to watch our favourite films and TV programmes. In due course, an intelligent machine learning algorithm will helpfully start recommending some content that will be to our liking.

Traditionally, the only way to get a computer to do something—from adding two numbers to flying an aircraft—was to write down an algorithm explaining how. Now, intelligent algorithms figure it out independently by making inferences from the data stored. The more data they have, the better they get. At present, there are no programming computers; they programme themselves.

All of us are already living with AI—an invisible pool of algorithm-powered machines analysing our life in between the time we wake up and the time we switch off our bedroom lights. Many functions that require human intervention are now automated by intelligent machines learning through algorithmic inputs about our mind! You eat breakfast and read the morning paper on your smartphone. The news that is updated in your notification tab is customized. So, you only see news that will interest you. Suppose sports and movies are the least interesting for you, but you like politics and tech news, so you will receive only those according to your tastes. An algorithm learns your news taste and even curates them for you!

Nest Thermostat is an AI-enabled, self-learning, Wi-Fi-enabled and energy-conserving machine that optimizes the heating and cooling of home and office spaces. The machine learns from how humans intervene in the regulation of heat as reference data in the initial weeks. The AI algorithm in the machine, in due course, learns each individual's schedule and the temperature each one of them maintains in the room. The machine shifts to energy-saving mode depending on each user's smartphone location and uses AI-powered sensors to figure out to switch on when people step into the room and switch off when nobody is home.[11]

At lunchtime, you walk down the street, smartphone in hand, looking for a place to eat. Yelp's learning system helps you find it.[12] If you want more AI-powered restaurant-locating apps, you can download Foursquare, Eat24, Zagat and others.[13] They are local-search services powered by crowd-sourced review forums.

Your cell phone has language-learning algorithms. They are hard at work correcting your typos, understanding your spoken commands and much more. Furthermore, AI-powered language apps can teach you a language in just a few hours, when it takes about 200 hours using traditional methods to gain basic proficiency in a new language. You also have AI-powered language-learning platforms, such as Busuu, Duolingo, Babbel, Memrise and Rosetta Stone for mobile. In the end, AI can replace a language teacher and translator.

Apps on your phone can even anticipate what you are going to do next and advise you accordingly. For example, as you are finishing lunch, it discreetly alerts you that your afternoon meeting with an out-of-town visitor will have to start late because the visitor's flight has been delayed. To help you in every way possible, there are AI-powered apps like MyKAI, Time, Trevor, LifeTracker, Talla, Focuster and others.

Night has fallen by the time you get off work. Machine learning helps keep you safe as you walk to your car, monitoring the video feed from the surveillance camera in the parking lot and alerting the off-site security staff if it detects suspicious activity. Your cameras are gaining intelligence. They can connect to the Wi-Fi and have 'minds' of their own. Google Clips, a miniature camera device released by Google, clips on whatever you would like and uses machine learning to automatically photograph what it 'thinks' would be of interest to you. The camera often responds to lighting, facial expressions and other common traits of good photos while photographing humans and pets. Google Clips isn't the only AI-powered camera drawing attention. In 2017, Lighthouse AI unveiled the Lighthouse security camera, which combines AI, a 24-hour video feed and up to a month of storage for footage to keep your home safe. A homeowner can ask the camera's AI to ping them if it sees an unfamiliar face or to let them know if anyone enters the house at an odd hour. In terms of spying, it could also be very easy for one member of a family to use Lighthouse's AI technology to spy on someone else in the house—to see if the kids have friends over, if a spouse is cheating or if their teens are sneaking out at night.

On your way home, you stop at an AI-powered supermarket, such as Watasale in Cochin, Kerala, modelled after Amazon Go. It is an autonomous store that works on computer vision with the right number of cameras. Deep learning is used to analyse the interaction between customers and the store. No cashier, no scanning and no waiting in line. You enter the store by scanning the QR code on Watasale's mobile app. After you have selected whatever you need, on your way out, the amount will be automatically debited from your credit/debit card or mobile wallet linked to the app. They also use big data analysis to optimize in-store customer experience. A learning algorithm decides to send you the offer for that card and in approving your application. Another algorithm continually looks for suspicious transactions and alerts you if it thinks your card details were stolen. A third one tries to estimate how happy you are with this card. If you are a good customer but look dissatisfied, you get an offer before switching to another one. But as AI-powered shopping experiences advance, you need not go to the supermarket in the future. AI-powered refrigerator and grocery shelves, which have machine learning functions, learn what to buy for you and places the order from the local supermarket.

Crime in your city is noticeably down since the police started using statistical learning to predict where crimes are most likely to occur and concentrating night patrols there. As you start to eat dinner with your family, the MLA is in the news—the one you voted for because he personally called you on election day, after a learning algorithm informed him that you were a key undecided voter.

Before going to sleep, you take your medicine, which was designed and tested with the help of WebMD AI doctor, which uses learning algorithms. WebMD is one of the most famous symptom-checking portals on the Internet. Your doctor, too, may have used machine learning to help diagnose you—from interpreting X-rays to figuring out an unusual set of symptoms. There are plenty of AI-powered doctor apps on the Internet you can download to your mobile phone, such as TalkLife, Ada, Babylon Health, K Health and SkinVision. Such apps ask simple, relevant questions and compare your answers to thousands of similar cases to help you find possible explanations for your symptoms. Platforms like SkinVision can help identify skin cancer early. They work on both iPhone and Android devices and instantly give you a diagnosis. These platforms are mining health-based big data to make their diagnoses more accurate. Their algorithms have already stored the health data of millions of people around the world. You just have to give answers to their queries, upon which they can predict what might be your case. And their predictions may be more accurate than a human doctor because they mine health data of millions of people to find possible matches for you. The more the data, the more accurate their predictions are.

This is your day in the life of machines with a brain. The story doesn't end with the day, however. All aspects of human life are now invaded by these machines with intelligence. The next time you apply for a job, think that a learning algorithm might have picked your résumé from the virtual pile and told your prospective employer, 'Here is a strong candidate, take a look'. AI seems to be taking the world of human resources (HR) and recruitment by storm. AI-powered assistants, also known as chatbots, are already in use for various aspects of HR and recruitments.

Mya is a leading conversational AI platform for hiring teams, which automates tedious parts of the recruitment process such as sourcing, screening and scheduling. It is powered by machine learning and uses natural language processing (NLP) to pick up on details that come up in conversation. Mya also creates candidate profiles and shortlists applicants. Another AI-driven chatbot,

Olivia, engages with candidates via various mobile platforms or social media channels. Just like her counterpart Mya, Olivia uses NLP and also handles the scheduling part of the recruitment process. Then there are services like Beamery, Textio, mroads and Harver, which use machine learning, data, predictive analytics and AI-powered video interviews for recruitment purposes.

If you are looking to buy a house, Zillow (zillow.com) will estimate the worth of each property you are considering. When you have settled on one, you apply for a home loan and a learning algorithm studies your application and recommends accepting it or not. With almost every sector embracing this technology with a lot of warmth, the real estate sector isn't lagging behind either. Property companies and reputed realtors across the world have come forward and integrated AI systems into their existing infrastructure, for example Altum AI (altum.ai), Localize (www.localize.city), Deepblocks (www.deepblocks.com), CoreLogic (www.corelogic.com) and Freshworks (www.freshworks.com). Commercial and residential buildings are becoming smarter with each passing day. So, using AI in your search for residential property, you can identify the temperature levels and energy consumption amounts—thus optimizing smart energy utilization. Timely fault detection leads to effective and preventive disaster management. Automated voice and facial recognition become easier with AI-enabled security systems in your residential area. If you are an agent, whenever a new property enthusiast visits your site, you will have to provide the right information or useful suggestions. With AI-powered site management systems, you can identify the information that is useful to them and make valuable recommendations. In the days to come, instead of hiring a real estate agent, you can essentially recruit a computer to sell your four-bedroom home in your city. To sell a home, algorithm-powered software disseminate an initial batch of ads based on a prediction about where and who the likely buyers are. If someone clicks on an ad, the software will tailor future ads for that individual based on the behaviour they have demonstrated on the website. The machine learning algorithm also identifies potential home buyers and sellers by gathering data from retailers and businesses that show changes in people's purchasing behaviour. It is common practice for companies to sell data about consumers' purchases to third parties and advertisers.

Perhaps most important, if you have used an online dating service, machine learning may even have helped you find the love of your life.[14] Forget swiping though endless profiles. Dating apps are using AI to suggest where to go on a first date, recommend what to say and even find a partner who looks like your favourite celebrity. Betterhalf (www.betterhalf.ai) is a matchmaking platform that uses AI to improve user experience. Online dating pioneer eHarmony announced that it is developing an AI-based feature. British dating app Loveflutter plans to use AI to analyse chats between its users to determine their compatibility and suggest when to meet. There is also a voice-operated dating app called AIMM which uses AI to mirror a human matchmaking service.

Society is changing, and AI is at the centre—renovating science, technology, business, politics and war. Self-learning machines are the newest chapter in the journey of humans with tools. The machine senses what you want and it adjusts accordingly, without your having to lift a finger. These seemingly magical technologies work, because at its core, a self-inventing machine is all about prediction: what are the results of your actions, predicting what you want, what you think, how you react and how to achieve your goals.

At the moment, all we can do is build machines that reproduce the way we think. We are not capable of teaching them what we ourselves don't know. But, ultimately, we may build machines that can go beyond us—intelligent enough to create machines of their own, without human intervention.

If no humans require them, machines don't have a reason to live in this world. Maybe they are self-learning for now so as to reinvent themselves in the future. Will they terminate themselves if humans don't need them anymore? Perhaps our generation is lucky (or unlucky) to be born early enough not to see all these forms of technological complexity.

# 2

# Cognitive Disaster

Emotions like curiosity (when you are going to watch a new movie), boredom (because you have a lecture you don't want to attend), sadness (because of a break-up), excitement (about weekend plans) and thrill (as there is a school project you enjoy) are all a part of human nature and allow us to react according to situations. We get better at knowing what we are feeling as we grow older, and we also learn why we feel it, with time. We can call this emotional awareness, which helps us talk about our emotions in words and communicate it effectively to other people. Humans are both skilled in expressing emotions and understanding the emotions of others. When someone smiles at you, you can read its meaning. You can also read when someone is angry at you without them having to physically express it.

To make survival easier as well as to focus on the more human aspects of our lives, humans have used machines. One important facet of the functioning of a machine is its efficiency. The more efficient it is, the more we appreciate it. Since the industrial revolutions, humans are increasingly preoccupied with efficiency. We are in search of machines that perform functions more efficiently than human capacity. Perhaps because of the emotional aspect, humans are unpredictable—making us a barrier to the efficient discharge of functions from flight operation and liver transplantation to processing loan applications and paying bills. Robots can perform better than humans in functions like sensing, thinking and action. Machines can cook, sew clothes, mow the grass, fight forest fires and even conduct funerals.[15]

But what happens when this efficiency begins invading our cognitive and emotional abilities? We never imagined what happens if machines acquire these skills. But this is not our future—it's our present. Machines are becoming intelligent, and technologies are increasingly taking over the emotional awareness of humans, which forms a part of our cognitive world of love, sympathy and bonding.

This machine intervention into our lives is visible in various activities that are essential for human connection. This comes with consequences at the economic and social level as well. How does this happen, and how do we handle this intervention?

## Virtual Dining

Online food delivery is a principal example of a traditional market being disrupted. The staggering entry of online food-delivery services has disrupted traditional food culture. Food-delivery apps provide extra channels for potential revenue; however, they also create the risk of destroying brick-and-mortar sales. Food-delivery apps are a specific type of online-to-offline (O2O) platform that leverages on consumers' wide-ranging use of mobile internet, connection devices and navigational services like GPS. Consumers who purchase in-store have migrated mostly to online purchasing activities. The Covid-19 pandemic has further hastened this trend because in-person dining has been greatly reduced. Reports even predict that online food delivery was one of the winners of the Covid-19 outbreak.[16]

But the story doesn't end there. O2O platforms have replaced an important human ability to relate with other humans, particularly when it comes to understanding the emotions of other people.

A time before online food platforms like Swiggy came into play, you had to go to a restaurant for an evening outing. You travel in your personal car or a hired cab on a busy road and see the world out of the car window. There are people around with various purposes—somebody is rushing home, while another is making household purchases. At the restaurant, you are greeted by the security at the door. You come across a lot of strangers and food lovers. The waiter takes your order. While the food is getting prepared, you engage in a lovely conversation with your family members or friends. You share the food with everyone instead of eating all by yourself. In the end, you give a tip to the service staff as a token of good service. While exiting, as the security personnel gives you directions for parking, you also give them a tip. Back at home, you will have a good feeling that you live in this world, where lots of people relate to you. This is one thing that makes us human. Research from the University of Oxford has reported people will feel happier and more satisfied when they eat often with other people. So, dining out has social utility. People are likely to have a wider social network which gives them emotional and social support. Eating with someone makes them feel closer to each other. Laughter and reminiscences occur while dining out, which helps them enhance the feeling of togetherness.[17]

In the case of online orders, a few clicks on the app downloaded on a smartphone and a delivery boy replaces all the social experience. The whole social world you have come across is suddenly shut down. Yet, we are happy that the food-delivery staff benefits from the new job possibilities that data companies have created. In the process of the Zomato boy picking up your order and delivering you the food, you can imagine a whole scenario of people connecting with other people.

But this possibility will not persist for long since tech giants are trying to develop drone delivery systems.[18] For many years, data giants such as Alphabet, Amazon and Uber have promised drone delivery systems, bringing goods to our doorsteps in a matter of minutes. Items, such as clothes, footwear, grocery items, books and other household products will be easily delivered by drones. It sounds like science fiction but will soon be a reality. When it happens, what will be the impact of replacing humans from a function we never thought machines would ever be able to perform? AI-enabled technologies will be all set to destroy the cultural foundation of our society. Your social world will eventually reduce to data. The problem is that this type of AI-enabled technology will destroy many vital aspects of our human world.

Crazy ideas are doing the rounds—driverless cars, image detection software, speech recognition, AI doctors and social robots. These ideas have already germinated from the confines of our imagination—some of them even possibly becoming tsunamis. Social robotics create machines that help humans just like all machines, but what makes these machines different from others is what or who they replace.

## There's No One behind the Wheel!

Santhosh is one of my friends who works as a driver for the public transport system run by the state of Karnataka. He got employed at the age of 23. He has seen endless people in his capacity as drivers to state-owned buses for the last 20 years. As he drives, he has seen the trust in many people's eyes showing that they believe their life is safe in his hands and the hope that he will take them to their destination. 'I remember the unexpressed love in many of my passengers' eyes when I drop them off at their destinations', he told me in a personal conversation. 'On their lips, they hide their gratitude, love and friendship', he continued. 'When I see them some other time in a passing crowd, their facial expressions give me the feeling that they still remember me.' He was talking like a successful person who grabbed people's appreciation. Of course, it was the love that made Santhosh a committed public servant for a lifetime. The satisfaction derived from an underpaid job is in the form of love. It educated him on the human skills of compassion, group behaviour, love and sympathy.

A few weeks back, as I talked to him, he had heard of driverless cars, but didn't know how they work. Driverless vehicles have escaped the confines of our imaginations and found their way on to our roadways. Major companies, including General Motors (GM), Nissan, Mercedes-Benz, Toyota, Lexus, Hyundai, Tesla, Uber and Volkswagen are all developing autonomous vehicles. Tech giant Google has reported that the development of autonomous vehicles is among its topmost business projects.

'What is the logic behind such vehicles?' Santhosh asked me, bewildered. 'It works on algorithms and AI,' I said. My reply didn't make any sense to him. Instead of asking me what these things are, he asked, 'Can it avoid collision and death in unforeseen accidents?' He looked like a child who was trying to know the secrets to how birds fly! I said, 'Yes, it can avoid death in unforeseen accidents.'

Suppose a driverless car with five passengers is heading for an imminent crash with a two-wheeler and a school bus and has to choose whether to first knock over a two-wheeler or crash head-on into a school bus with 20 school children.[19] If it hits the school bus head-on, it will kill all five passengers. However, the driverless car predicts the casualty of the crash using different scales and indicates other possibilities. Then by design, it tries to minimize the casualty. This is possible at the intersection of multiple technical know-hows. AI replaces the role of cognitive abilities that the drivers have been using at the millionth of a second to avoid a crash. Machine learning gets insight into human intentions across all roadways, and the Internet of things (IoT) is brought in for generating predictions on how most of us are conducting almost all aspects of our life over the Internet. This generates a huge volume of data that the human brain cannot process instantly. AI works as intelligently as human brains to predict and analyse situations so that it can reduce crashes and keep casualties to the minimum. Using prediction technology, the driverless vehicle decides to collide with the school bus. It can swerve so that it first collides into the two-wheeler, thus lessening the impact on the school bus. This would spare the 20 children on the school bus, but it would, unfortunately, kill the two people on the two-wheeler. Should the driverless vehicle be programmed to first crash into the two-wheeler?

It also raises a question: who should choose the ethics for the autonomous vehicle—drivers, consumers, passengers, manufacturers, programmers or politicians? Earlier, it was the cognitive ability of a driver that took the decision at the blink of an eye. Now, the driver's cognitive abilities have been taken over by AI; and in its place, machine learning holds sway.[20] The human side of our life is, thus, lost to this type of social robotics.

## Intelligent Machines Even Shape Human Sexuality

Venkatesh Reddy, who was employed in a tech company in Cyberabad told me in a friendly conversation, 'I am addicted to porn sites. I got erectile dysfunction, so I needed stimulants. My wife doesn't allow me to watch it.' He waved his head towards the window and continued, 'I have been frequenting tube sites since my college days. But that was all fun.' I asked, 'Are you not attracted to girls?' He nodded. 'I am, but it doesn't feel natural when I am intimate with my partner.'

Venkatesh is not alone in feeling like this. Sex is a very personal and intimate experience. Personalization of the experience is important here. Tube sites operate well in this territory, but in the future, it will redefine the rules of user experience—because the porn industry is very tech savvy. Tube sites have conquered Venkatesh's natural human sexual drive and automated his intimate life. In place of his natural human desires and the sensual aspects of life, machine learning has already taken control.[21] For example, tube sites use algorithms and machine learning to recommend content specific to a user, just like video-streaming sites do. An AI algorithm examines their browsing history, the machine learning systems learn their preference, the genre they like and so on, and from the thousands of videos in their database, they can recommend the most suitable ones. So, data giants have the power to easily track, control and shape a user's sexual behaviour.

Data giants want to tailor their advertisements to the user's tastes and habits. As the user visits tube sites frequently, Google tracks their behaviour and shows ads accordingly on adult websites—through the browser cookies and bots already installed in his connection devices. The moment the user comes across any content, the data is shared with every interested stakeholder.

But Google is not the only platform that tracks what you are doing alone at midnight. PornHub, the popular tube site, has a cool feature. It tries to improve the personalization experiences of its users. Instead of analysing the categories its users love, PornHub is now using innovated technology to predict which part of a video one is interested in viewing and which part one skipped. This information is later used to recommend content.[22] You may have successfully hidden your late-night viewing habits from your partner. However, Facebook could be watching everything you do, thanks to its clever web-tracking technology.

For example, suppose you spend an inordinate amount of time looking for your favourite porn star. In that case, Facebook will incorporate this into its profile for you and might start to show you ads. Facebook actively tracks all your online search behaviour. When you are surfing tube sites for pornography, Facebook can collect data about the websites you have visited if you are logged into Facebook in one the browsers on your device. You are probably not too bothered that Facebook knows you watch porn. But these 'Like, Share and Login with Facebook' prompts can also track a number of online habits you would rather keep private.[23]

From one such ad, Venkatesh came to know more about sex toys that can be bought online. But this business operates secretly. Such devices are considered unnatural in India, but he managed to own one, and now is an avid user of sex toys. It makes him feel natural and efficient using them. 'You can use it whenever you need, no time lapses waiting for a physical partner,' he says. 'Now there are talks about human-size sex robots, which can replace a human partner.' Sex toys have already replaced physical sex in his life, and in its place, he has already started imagining smart machines that can be remotely operated.

## Professor AI

Imagine this scenario: Sriram Shivamani, a student sitting in a hot classroom, was feeling sleepy. He logged into YouTube and found educational content created by professional agencies and universities in which the topic discussed in the class was better-narrated, with easily understandable illustrations. In the comment thread, there were plenty of discussions in which the speakers themselves had replied to all the questions. The interaction seemed more engaging than the physical classroom engagements. Why then attend dry lectures when high-quality educational content is available in plenty and being circulated in other easily available channels? In this way, educational content being created in data formats can easily replace physical classrooms and engagements.

The sad side of this shift would be the loss of cognitive skills you get from physical classrooms. Love and failures, emotions, relationships, conversations, connection, understanding—these will be replaced by data. Among all the areas where AI will have an impact, the biggest will be in education. Flipped classrooms and online learning have already transformed the education system—where the possibilities of AI are more competent than the features of traditional classrooms. AI will take over, at an increasing scale, classroom activities from teaching, writing, assignments, seminars, examination, and even some extent of tuition and coaching. Virtual and augmented reality makes history lessons of World War I more of a personal experience; a chemistry teacher explains the molecular structure of water more personally through the virtual reality (VR) model.

## Talk to Your Phone

The other day, my friend Revathy Manoj used the voice search feature on Google for the best tour spots in Mysore. Google accurately typed out what she had uttered. She was impressed. The same words were typed within the blink of an eye, and Google listed the search results accordingly. Google Voice Search is a Google product that allows users to use the search function on a mobile phone or computer through speech. If you have a social anxiety disorder or suffer from a fear of being watched or judged, the best place to find a location, a shop or tourist destination is through voice search. It's your best friend during such times, one that you can talk to. It will type for you and give directions and answers quicker than any human being. It seems a useful tech tool for Revathy, as her natural shyness prevents her from connecting with strangers. She doesn't need to talk to strangers for any help in identifying a location or place. Voice search is a fantastic tech feature that connects her to the world.

The prediction analytics is really accurate on Google. However, this type of data companies deprive Revathy of connecting with real people. As you need to talk to people for enquiring about directions to a place, the natural human instinct for connection comes into play automatically.

## The Death of Humans

Similarly, AI replaces many things related to our cognitive skills. A robot walks alongside human workers at a supermarket, perhaps other robots as well. It watches as the human worker demonstrates how to perform a particular task, and then it expertly takes over the job. At the multiplex theatre in your hometown, a robot with a mechanical smile and friendly voice persuades a child to sip on bottled milk, and then turns to other toddlers in the play area.

What if robots remind your mother of her blood pressure medicine and your father of his cholesterol tablets, which usually you have to do?

What if you are reminded by a robot of your morning schedule, which your wife does every day?

What if your electricity bill, phone bill, newspapers bill, milk bill and others are paid by way of social robotics?

This type of assistance by mechanization seems like a pretty good idea at first, but deeper behind it exists the real danger—the death of humans!

Our generation will certainly not experience the ripple effects of AI as grave as our children's generation. But the sad side of this shift will be in their children's generation. For their generation, tech will be the new normal. They will never know that their parents went to restaurants in the local town in the evening with their parents and had lovely family dinners full of conversation and fun. They talked to strangers in the local streets and shared the camaraderie of community living. They travelled a long distance to pay the electricity bills and telephone bills.

## Do We Really Understand Technology?

My wife Gayu has developed a curiosity about a lot of tech novelties currently in vogue: AI, social robotics, predictive algorithms, social analytics, IoT, big data, data mining, drone delivery systems, driverless cars, AI doctor and machine learning. But she is not very familiar with these technical terms, and she isn't the only one, as most of us don't know what they mean. We rarely get a chance to understand the nuances of any technology, even when most of us benefit from them.

The problem with intelligent machine technologies is the old human irony. Only a handful of people invented the most important technologies which brought tectonic shifts in history; the rest of us have benefited fundamentally from these technologies without realizing the meaning of the inventions. Most people don't even know how electricity, automobile engines or telephones work. But all of us use them. Even though our society is extremely dependent on science and technology, hardly anyone knows anything about either.

As I told all this to Gayu, she started looking through the window of our reading room. Stars could be seen beyond the trees. They winked at her. Soon, she called her mother over the phone and talked for half an hour for no reason, without any predetermined topic. They talked about the neighbour's daughter's dance classes and Gayu's childhood. Sometimes, they even paused for minutes—that itself formed their conversation. I listened to their conversation without distraction till the end. Still, our cognitive power remains with us! Doesn't it?

# 3

# Intelligent Machines Will Conquer Us

There is a huge possibility that you have interacted with AI with or without knowing. This is because AI is used everywhere, including on your computer, in analysing behaviour on CCTV, in underlining search engines, and, last but not least, in the functioning of financial markets.

AI is the concept of rendering human-like intelligence to a machine or, more broadly, to all forms of matter! To understand it, let us imagine that the human brain is made broadly of three important functions: storing, computing and learning. If so, anything that performs these functions attains intelligence. We use matter to compute, store and learn. Once we are able to combine all these human abilities together into tangible forms, natural intelligence can be artificially created. Hence, the term 'artificial intelligence'. This concept now reigns supreme everywhere in our world.

From autonomous cars replacing human drivers and centralized AI cameras replacing human security staff, AI is all around us. These developments have been made possible by a host of emerging technologies that automate physical tasks (robotics), intellectual tasks (cognitive computing) and customer service tasks (everything from self-help kiosks to grocery store scanners). Such technologies are intelligent, performing similarly to humans. Let us see how these technologies are different from those this far.

## How Does the Machine Learn?

To make any machine system work, you must build a set of instructions that tells it exactly what to do. This is called the code. Here, you must carefully define every input because machines cannot figure out things on their own. Imagine that if a single comma or dot is missing in the thousands of lines of input code, the entire machine programming will crash. In such occasions, a person must intervene, identify the missing input and insert it. This process is called debugging.

So, let us look at it this way: why can't machines do this process themselves? It is only possible by way of learning. Learning in machine systems is the ability to analyse new scenarios and adapt to changing situations. But is it not found only in intelligent living creatures? Thus enters machine learning, which tries to gain insights into new situations and predict behaviour. Machine learning is functioning on algorithms. An algorithm processes data and finds patterns, structures and conclusions. Data is a very important property for AI, and AI algorithms need to first process a huge stockpile of data with enough variety to perform specific functions. Machine learning can use algorithms, thereby acquiring the cognitive ability to compute and learn from scenarios. It receives and analyses input data to predict output values within an acceptable range. That means this type of machine system develops 'intelligence' over time.

In simple terms, AI is the capability of any form of matter to mimic intelligent human behaviour.

## A Brief History of AI

The concept of inanimate or lifeless matter-forms becoming intelligent has existed since the era of ancient Egyptians, Chinese and Greeks. For example, the ancient Egyptians and Chinese had built automatons—a moving mechanical device created analogous to a human being; and the Greeks had myths about robots. The Greek myth of Pandora and her infamous box of chaos is an example of intelligent thinking machines.[24] The conceptual root of modern-day AI goes all the way back to the classical Greek thinkers' attempt to describe human thinking as a symbolic system. Aristotle's syllogisms led to symbolic logic, which in turn has led to machines learning and thinking.

In 11 February 1737, the French mechanical genius Jacques de Vaucanson created a statue that played music from a flute.[25] It was a wonder machine that could play music just like humans, and it made the European scientists think about machines performing functions without human intervention, thus the idea of intelligence that is created artificially.

Thinking machines are therefore not new. We have been trying to build computers and machines that exhibit some level of human intelligence for many decades since the 1950s. In the 1940s, Grey Walter, a researcher at the University of Bristol, UK, created an autonomous mechanical turtle that moved and reacted to light and even learn.[26] In 1950, Alan Turing, the famous British scientist even argued that one day machines would think like humans. He had the opinion that if one day, a computer is capable of engaging in conversation with a human, then we could conclude that the computer thinks. This thought later became the famous Turing test—a test of a machine's ability to exhibit behaviour as intelligent as humans. The ideas of Alan Turing shaped our progress to create thinking machines.

Despite Turing and others whose ground-breaking thoughts laid the foundation of artificially created intelligence, the term 'artificial intelligence' goes back to American computer scientist John McCarthy, who coined the term at the second Dartmouth

Conference in 1956. AI simulates intelligent behaviour from computer-controlled machines or digital computers. It gives a machine the ability to carry out tasks normally associated with intelligent beings like us. However, by the 1980s, scientists realized that computers cannot do everything that humans do. So, instead of moving to one single general human intelligence, scientists are now focussing on specific functions—image recognition, speech recognition, computer visions and even chess. Each of these sub fields of AI has been successful. For example, IBM developed Deep Blue, a computer which beat Garry Kasparov, the world champion in chess. The problem with this type of specific and narrow range of expertise was that it could play chess, recognize speech or image but could not discuss strategies it had employed in a situation nor perform other functions. By the 1990s, it became clear that nobody was making great leaps in pushing AI.

Subsequent research in the fields such as generic algorithms and artificial neural networks were developed, which imitate the way neurons function in the human brain. The development of these new approaches increased hope. The increase of the stock of intelligence artificially means a revolution in the way human beings see the world. While some people falsely consider AI as a technology, it is appropriate to see it as a broader concept. Machines, driven by AI, are able to deal with tasks in a way we would call intelligent.

## Machine Intelligence: Types of AI

As we know, intelligence is often understood as the ability to solve problems in an efficient way. It is called the ability to compute and analyse. Intelligence also requires the ability to learn and memorize. Learning can be defined as a process to gain knowledge. Memory is the ability to store the knowledge gained. To solve problems efficiently, humans need to learn and memorize. Knowledge is stored in the memory and human intelligence has the ability to process the knowledge stored according to situations. As of now, these functions are already gained by machines at various levels. But even in that framework of thinking, what machines still lack is the ability to interpret subjective experiences and cognition, which are deeply connected to human intelligence.[27]

There are certain things a machine or computer programme must be able to do to be called an AI. A computer cannot be considered an intelligent machine only because it performs certain functions it has already been programmed to do. First, it should be able to process and mimic the human capacity to think. Second, it should act human-like—intelligent, rational and ethical.

It is also important to make sense that the AI concept relates to weak AI and general AI. Weak AI exists in computers nowadays. It is taught or made to learn how to carry out specific tasks without being programmed specifically for that task, such as voice and image recognition, as discussed earlier. These AI are termed narrow because they can only learn how to do a specific task. Narrow AI can do things like respond to simple customer-service queries or book a hotel room at the right price and location. It can help radiologists spot potential cancer tumours in X-rays, detect wear and tear in elevators, flag improper content online to guard viewers, and hundreds more.

General AI, on the other hand, is an entirely different entity. It has a similar adaptable brain capability found in human beings and has an intellect that outperforms the cognitive skills of humans in all domains. This ease of action allows them to learn how to achieve different goals, such as building spreadsheets, social robotics which can take care of your grandparents, haircutting, autonomous driving, delivering food to your doorstep using drones, assessing your physical fitness and bring paradigm shifts in the healthcare industry. So far, it does not exist, and AI experts are divided over when it will be a reality. According to a couple of surveys, groups of experts reported some chance that artificial general intelligence (AGI) would develop around 2040 or 2050.[28] The chances are higher by 2075. The emergence of super-intelligence is predicted in other surveys. A couple of years after the development of AGI, super-intelligence may be a possibility.

At present, AI is used in a variety of fields, such as machine learning, cognitive computing, deep learning, predictive application, NLP and speech recognition. In recent years, AI has garnered attention from the major tech giants of the world, such as Google, Apple, Facebook, Amazon and IBM.

## The AI Industry

The AI industry may be divided into three domains: AI platform developers, AI enablers and AI products and services. An AI platform developer, as the name suggests, develops the AI software and applications that a particular business may be interested in. They programme systems and solutions that will best suit the needs of businesses based on the data collected and analysed. Platform developers often work with machine learning engineers, data engineers and data scientists. Google Cloud AI, Amazon AI services, Microsoft Azure AI, IBM Watson Studio, Wipro Holmes AI and automation platform are some examples.

The development of AI requires enablers. Data infrastructure, high-speed broadband, governance and regulations, funding and investments, research and academia, the private sector, the civil society, and developing skills and education can boost AI applications.[29] AI products and services are an important layer in the development of AI. There are key areas where AI is great in demand, such as manufacturing robots, self-driving cars, automated financial investing, NLP tools and virtual travel booking agents.

## Machine Beats Man!

Answers are divided on the question, 'Can machines act as intelligent as humans?' Arguments take one form or another, leading them to one kind of dualist or non-dualist view.[30] These debates gained importance in recent years as there have been some success in building machines that perform specific brain functions—such as speech recognition, image recognition and analysis. The problem is exacerbated when some scientists claim a new future generation of machines and robots which would overtake human capabilities.

Are these founded on unnecessary anxiety or misinterpretations of existing scenarios? To overcome human thinking abilities, machines and computers require a set of distinctive processes and characteristics which define being a human, such as abstract thinking, intelligence, the creation of art and music, language capability, managing emotions and physical abilities, among others. We know that the idea of creating machines with human-like intelligence has gained currency since the 1950s, and a singular form of human intelligence was the focus of computer scientists. But by the 1980s, due to AI winter—a period of reduced funding and interest in AI research produced by over-inflated promises by developers—there was a growing sense that machines could not attain human-like intelligence.

But there is a growing understanding that computers, machines and robots will eventually reach or even overtake human intelligence in the future. Most probably the case that we are still not ready to accept it, but there will be a point in the future when AI will overtake the human race when it comes to specific functions. AI has already started off better than humans by beating us in games invented by us. Some of the smartest humans in the world of professional gaming have already been defeated by AI machines. Deep Blue, a chess-playing computer developed by scientists at IBM, beat Kasparov by forcing him to resign by Game 6 on 11 May 1997—just after 19 moves.[31]

The Ancient Chinese game of 'Go' is considered more sophisticated than chess, which makes its players some of the smartest people in the world. In the Google DeepMind Challenge match, a five-game Go match between AlphaGo, a computer Go programme developed by Google DeepMind, and 18-time world champion Lee Sedol, played between 9 and 15 March 2016, AlphaGo became champion. AlphaGo went on to beat the next-four top players in the world. Libratus, an AI, in 2017, managed to beat four professional poker players at the same time in a no-limit Texas Hold'em poker game, which is a highly psychological game that requires players to read the mind of their opponent. DeepMind, AlphaGo and Libratus are a few examples to highlight the prophecy that, in the future, AI can achieve human intelligence.[32]

The beginning of this hope was seen in the 1990s. Computer scientists and tech developers shifted their attention from general intelligence to narrow intelligence. Robots that have passed some kind of self-consciousness test remain a hope for scientists that machines can attain consciousness.[33]

## Doomsday Scenario

The situation seems to be such that those who understand the full potential of AI are more scared of it than those who only know the basics. Employees of Google demanded that the company stop work on a project for the Pentagon. There was fear that the company was working in the business of war. The project was originally planned to use AI to make it easier to classify images of people and objects shot by drones.[34]

One day, not only will AI exceed human performance, but it will also extend beyond human control. So many fearful articles out there warn us of the apocalyptic turn of AI. There are questions like 'Is artificial intelligence safe?' 'Are humans being replaced by artificial intelligence' or 'Is artificial intelligence bad for people?'—which should come as no surprise.

Given the innate advantage AI machines have over us humans, an AI rebellion scenario is something we should not completely dismiss. Time will show whether AI is our greatest existential threat or a blessing that will improve our quality of life.

The decline in human social interaction may become a problem. If you look at AI as a broad concept from the perspective of how technology could be used to mechanically replace humans in a variety of duties, the human aspect of our social life will be reduced to a bare minimum. There will be bizarre scenarios—matrimonial algorithms replacing traditional marriage brokers, AI doctors minimizing the role of physical doctors or even making them extinct, writing by hand replaced by voice-typing algorithms, AI-curated newspaper columns on online news feeds replacing your favourite columnists, AI news replacing the news industry itself, sex robots replacing human sexual interaction, predictive algorithms replacing human emotions, AI technologies reducing your social connections by way of bringing almost all your requirements to your doorstep and drones replacing your delivery boys.

Robots and AI are two separate things but can be combined for a good purpose. Robots are mechanized bodies while AI is the non-physical part. AI is essentially the brain, although using the term 'brain' is a loaded approach—as AI can't currently think like a human. Instead, it learns from data, analysing the input it has been given, seeking patterns and generating new insights. Robots and AI are becoming more integrated into our everyday lives, and will replace us from many human-only functions in the future.

But by that time, the grandchildren of your grandchildren will be young adults or adults. Yes, there will no longer be any writers whom we adore and celebrate. There will not be any human sporting icons that we post on our WhatsApp status or Facebook timeline, celebrate and worship. There will no longer be music composed by humans, as intelligent technologies can mimic the natural voice in a way far better than humans. Nor will there be any human-created artwork, as intelligent machines can copy the art style of even Leonardo da Vinci, Picasso and Michelangelo. Nor will there be any human doctors whom we get to consult after a long queue in their busy clinics. There will no longer be any film actors—intelligent animation robots can recreate your most favourite actors digitally. AI is expected to master all the vital human skills in the future. That also means that instead of machines and AI becoming more human, humans are, too, becoming more robotic.

So far, one thing remains perfectly clear. AI is one of the most remarkable innovations for humankind. We have had three western industrial revolutions in the modern age. The first was the advent of the steam-powered mills, and the second was steel, oil and electrical power. The most recent one, the third, is the digital revolution, a product of the Internet and the personal computer. We are now, as is said, on the brink of the fourth industrial revolution—where AI and robotics disrupt and replace our existing means of production. A major component of the fourth industrial revolution, the socio-economic impact of AI, is as huge as the invention of electricity and steam engine once had.

In this background, the smartest approach would be to keep an eye on how the technology takes shape, take advantage of the improvements it brings to our lives and not get too nervous at the thought of a machine takeover. Instead, be cautious!

# 4

# Attention for Sale

As I scroll down my Facebook feed, automobile ads from brands such as Jeep India, Skoda, Volkswagen appear frequently. When I click on the ad page, my details are already available on their feedback form. How do they know I plan to buy a new car? Industry prediction has been streamlined as such that they would get access to every detail about my personal life, sometimes even beyond. This type of ad-targeting strategy might shape my whole consumer behaviour. The purpose of this ad is to seek the attention of users of digital media platforms, which offer free services like email, uploads and posts.

Automobile commercials are not the only ad content that frequently appears on my Facebook timeline. The other day, I happened to see Amazon recommending books. Myntra, the online shopping site, recommends clothes. Sometimes, I even see online news platforms like *Scroll.in* and *The Wire* appear on my timeline. The Facebook algorithm tracks as much information as possible about me and you. Data giants like Facebook likely influence consumer behaviour. It simply means that brands collaborate with these data giants to market what they want to sell a consumer, which, by all possible means, they are able to do.

We often wonder how digital platforms like Facebook, Amazon and YouTube profit when their services are free. Most of us send emails, upload video content, share photos and transfer files free of charge. Of course, some kinds of investments require third parties to provide services. But they are not directly charging for their services. For example, we use the services of Oyo, Zomato, Flipkart and plenty others for free. But majority of us use their services without knowing how we pay them. Hence, it is important to understand how tech companies earn their revenues.

Let us consider the tagline of Facebook. For several years, its tagline was 'It's free and always will be', but now it has changed to 'It's quick and easy'.[35] Facebook was making a reference to the fact that it costs nothing to become a user. Twitter uses the tagline 'What's happening', whereas for more than 2 billion people in over 180 countries, the tagline for WhatsApp is 'With WhatsApp, you'll get fast, simple, secure messaging and calling for free, available on phones all over the world.' Both Twitter and WhatsApp make references to the idea that you can share content, connect with friends, and know what's happening all around the world. Emphasis goes to the concept 'free', meaning you don't need to pay for the services.

Most tech services, like Facebook, available for free on the web, are commoditizing the Internet and its users without seeking their prior approval. Most of the sites we visit, whether it is Amazon or Google, treat us not as customers or users. We are their products! We are participating in an intelligently crafted tech trap, which can be referred to as a feel-good euphemism titled 'The Attention Economy'.[36]

The clicks, hashtags and smileys result from the same market logic. They form what may be called a computational value. These expressions on digital platforms are not simply our conscious behaviour. Our actions are shaped intentionally by market logic created by tech firms. They are of immense computational value—leading to commoditizing our life. Our activities on these platforms are reduced to quantifiable numbers or calculations. So, the more you give time to a product, service offered, an idea or any other label of a tech brand, the better your prospects as a computational value in the market. The more you engage, the more you make a decision. This way, the attention you give to tech brands is making you their product.

Attention manipulation by businesses is hardly a new thing. We can find ample evidence that advertising-based business models have been used to sell products more profoundly than those selling without ads. However, the twenty-first-century business model of profit-for-your-eyeball is causing a big transformation to not only the way we do business but the way we live. Tech brands are shaping our decisions even without knowledge of the transformation we are in. Our life is consciously shaped by tech firms according to the attention we are giving them.

Recently, works like *The Costs of Connection: How Data Is Colonizing Human Life and Appropriating It for Capitalism* by Nick Couldry and Ulises A. Mejias, *Stand out of Our Light: Freedom and Resistance in the Attention Economy* by James Williams, and *The Age of Surveillance Capitalism* by Shoshana Zuboff inform us of the darker shades of tech stories. These books warn us of the market logic in which our value is reduced to the attention we are giving to tech brands like Facebook and YouTube. Movies such as *A.I Artificial Intelligence* or *The Great Hack* have shown us the hollowness of tech taglines like 'It's quick and easy' and 'fast, simple, secure messaging and calling for free'. Prof. Stephen Hawking told the BBC, 'The development of full artificial intelligence could spell the end of the human race.'[37] Computer security expert Bruce Schneier says, 'Don't make the mistake of thinking you're Facebook's customer, you're not—you're the product. Its customers are the advertisers.'[38] These warnings are just the tip of the iceberg. We are becoming data, our life has been reduced to attention we give to tech platforms, but all this is happening without our knowledge or approval. We never know how tech companies manipulate our attention.

## What Is Attention Economy?

Now, it is time to think about attention economy and make sense of how attention is the new market. The formal psychological and popular understanding of attention is simple. It may be referred to as selective focus on some of the mental stimuli humans are currently in, while ignoring all other stimuli. Psychologist and philosopher, William James, in his 1890 book titled *The Principles of Psychology*, says that 'It implies withdrawal from some things in order to deal effectively with others.'[39]

If you give attention to something, you have used up your mental resources so that you have less available resources to spend elsewhere. The many theories on human attention agree that attention is limited in scope. According to the psychologist and economist Herbert A. Simon, it is a 'bottleneck' in human thought. He also noted that 'a wealth of information creates a poverty of attention.'[40] It is generally believed that people can't multitask because they will lose attention on something. You may be scrolling on your phone while you watch the news on television, but you will certainly miss some of what is reported in the news.

The attention we are discussing in the attention economy is different from the popular notions of attention. It refers to the deliberate attempt through technology to find a market in our attention to something. Attention as a resource is valued by the corporate world, tech firms, businesses, even political campaigns and non-profits, along with plenty of organizations. They all try to entice us into spending our time on what they have to offer.

Simon was the first to propose the concept of attention economics.[41] In the 1990s, writers such as Thomas H. Davenport and Michael Goldhaber adopted terms like 'attention economy' and 'economics of attention' to explain that the global economy is shifting from a material-based economy to one based on the capacity of human attention.[42] From finding jobs and ordering grocery items to applying for a degree certificate and travelling to holiday destinations, these free services provided by tech companies everywhere have become our intimate companion. What makes these possible is just a simple logic: attention!

Attention was a resource and a currency even traditionally for business models. Attention economics, in the conventional sense, treats the attention of a potential customer as a resource. The model followed by advertisers who appeal to attention suggested a linear process, what they have called AIDA—attention, interest, desire and action. Tech firms today are able to run their organizations not because they have strong material wealth, but a huge catalogue of intangible resources. Now AIDA is challenged by millions of choices presented to the consumer. Moreover, users themselves are products for attention merchants.

Aspects like immediacy, personalization, interpretation, authenticity, accessibility, embodiment, patronage and findability makes companies run their organizations. Attention economy is not addressing our physical and material needs, but it targets our mental processes. So, needs, thoughts, feelings and emotions are created. You are now more likely to buy something even if you don't need it. You are now more likely to travel to a holiday destination even if you don't want to. You are more likely to watch a movie or buy a book even if you don't really need it. Attention economy creates a feeling of immediacy that you may think, 'Yes, I need it.' It gives you a feeling that you are making the best choice and that this particular thing is authentic even if it is not. The reason is that the attention economy is working on your mental processes. You can feel that this market is embodied in the books you buy, the movies you watch and the entertainment you are experiencing. You are patronized by the attention economy because you are more likely to think that it seems good, so I need it. And above all, everything is findable. There are many films, apps, songs, books and millions of other things—every second, appealing to your attention.

In the attention economy, you will get a platform and a service, free of cost, but you certainly pay for the services another way—attention is the currency.[43] We need to have a basic grip on the intricacies of this market pattern in which we are becoming a product. Attention economy operates in a complex system of a man–machine interface. Making sense of it requires thinking beyond what is taken for granted.

## Delivering Food by Grabbing Your Attention

If you are an undergraduate from a college in the countryside but migrated to an urban area in search of a job, a smartphone and a two-wheeler, along with fluency in English, are your best bets for a job in the tech-shaped new world. For example, you can very soon get employed by the online food-delivery platform Zomato. This data-aggregation platform is free to download on your smartphone device. It is easy for you to get employed in an online food-delivery platform—which, in fact, neither cooks the food nor sells products but simply gives you a free platform that functions on millions of users' attention.

Immediacy, patronage and findability work if you are an employer and you have orders online by users of Zomato. Doorstep delivery is what makes online food-delivery merchants special. The social system is fast-changing in the city. People are increasingly buying food online. That also means some forces from remote places can also influence your food culture. This is a competitive market and competition is made tough by other similar players. What is essential for them is to get the right buyer attracted to their platform within the blink of an eye. How to get the buyer's attention is important. Building an environment where the Zomato platform gets huge traffic in cyberspace is then their priority.

This is same with business models which use food data and eating habits of people for building a market. Download the app from an app store and register your details on the app. Select the menu to place an order for food to be delivered to your doorstep. That is all about this market. There are plenty of online food apps. Swiggy, Zomato, Uber Eats, foodpanda, Domino's, Pizza Hut, JustEat, and Faaso's are a few worth mentioning. The market for food-data apps is growing along with how society is fast changing. These attention merchants shape our food culture, buying behaviour and even social relationships without our knowledge. This is one form of the emerging attention economy which builds attention as its business resource.

## Cabs from an App

Another aspect being changed by the attention economy is transport. There is a market for online data-based cabs. If you are in need of a job and the only skill you have to offer is driving, the best choice given to you by the attention economy is online cab-data aggregation platforms. Cab-data aggregators are digital mediators or marketplaces for passengers to connect online with a driver for the intent of transportation. If you are introduced to the Uber platform, you can easily become an Uber driver if you have a commercial driving license and a police verification certificate and some other basic documents. Your vehicle must be a commercial vehicle (yellow plate) and in good condition. Most importantly, you should have an iOS or Android phone, which supports the Uber partner app. And you are set. These cab aggregators use technology and the attention economy to disrupt the existing system of taxi services and radio-taxi operators to help customers connect with all types of cabs and car rentals online. Cab aggregation is a business model innovated by the attention economy and was accelerated by the surge in smartphones and with the wider use of digital payment options.[44]

The market is tough. The point is how you seek the attention of a maximum number of clients a day. Since this market is replete with plenty of players, the first criterion is to push your platform visibility to as many people as possible. Seeking attention is decisive for this economic model to survive. Uber, Ola, Meru Cabs, EasyCabs, TaxiForSure, Savaari, Mega Cabs, TABcab, Wings Radio Cabs, CelCabs, Star Taxi and City Cool Cab are a few to mention. Big players dominate the market. If you are living in a big city, then a few of them will be available in your city, but if you live in tier 2 or tier 3 cities, then you will have only two to three or fewer options. This market works only on attention. More the attention you draw from the travel culture of people, the more the market grows! More players will come into the competition. The price decreases and users increase. Buying your attention to cab-data service is the key to this market.

## Grabbing the Attention of Readers

There is also a book-attention market. In the bygone days, books were sold because of the recommendations you received from those who had bought and read it. That also meant only good books were sold. Now, the market is different. Even bad books can be sold in plenty and good books can get lost. Attention economy is central to this new market. The more attention you draw from book readers for bad books, more the sale.

The attention economy operates more profoundly on Amazon. If you are book-savvy, you will find that many times, Amazon book ads pop up on your Facebook timeline. Occasionally, it drops emails in your inbox about books on its listings. Interestingly, the books you see on the list are closely related to the book themes you might have searched on Amazon. The site knows how you give attention to books, how you search and on what type of books you may give attention to in the future. Indeed, the platform predicts your reading habits and suggests books accordingly.

There is big competition for grabbing your attention in the book market. Findability, authenticity and reachability makes attention more demanding. This business model generates maximum user data, build an attention economy and find buyers. This is the way the book-data market works. There are many players, and if you want to buy books, you may go to Amazon, Flipkart, SnapDeal, BooksMela, EduCreon, just to mention a few. They try to grab your attention as much as possible.

## The Data Market

Google, Facebook and other data giants have information about your taste, habits, political views, likes and dislikes, what you are looking for, ideology, party affiliation and other things. They have a tremendous volume of data on you. An active presence in cyberspace gives you huge success in the offline market. So, app developers and companies track user data and archive it. Over a period of time, they collect a lot of user data. By roping in data analytics, they predict our behaviour. Accordingly, they notify frequently on our smartphone apps and other devices. A huge market like this has already grown in our country. This market prevails over almost everything in our social world. Our choices, decisions and needs are not conscious but shaped by the data aggregators which offer you the deals which we think is best for us. But it's a myth, an illusion. We are simply their products.

## AI in the Service of the Data Market

The selling point of this new market is our attention. These platforms can survive only if they get our attention. The first thing they must do then is to distract us. AI can best serve this function. They will give us a new brain, a new way of thinking and a new mind.

Between what we buy and what is listed for sale, the important thing is that moment in which clients take a decision. What better way than AI to influence it? It is simply not about attention anymore. It is beyond what we see. It is the logic of the attention economy: to control and shape our behaviour, especially our buying behaviour.

The new market works by way of enslaving us to technology platforms which use attention-seeking AI. Attention economy is built on our distraction. We are distracted from relationships, thoughts, people, emotions, etc. AI is the key to its functioning. It enslaves us by controlling our thoughts, defining our taste and instilling new habits in us. Finally, it will replace human elements, making us more like machines that can be operated with remote controls. Companies indeed hold the key to our cognitive mind. Data controls behaviour, and these companies control the data. Those who own data shape our behaviour, decisions and choices.

To understand this, we need to look at a bit of history. While the industrial age looked for consumers, the information age looks for users. Data is self-generated and self-marketed. No companies invest in manufacturing data. We users generate it. But this data that is so unimportant for us is very important for data firms. Those making predictions by gathering data about us indeed control the rest of us. It seems a weird idea but that is just what it is.

We are unknowingly becoming a product in a bigger story. As we become a product, the whole foundation of our life as an individual with cognitive capabilities gets reshaped. The impact is so profound that in the days to come, we as a consumer will no longer be a free-thinking, independent and autonomous human being with critical insight into the buried story of things.

From cab services and food to movies and books, our world is moving towards an attention-based economic model where decisions are not conscious but forces unknown to us that shape what we want, see, watch, eat, read and so on. Attention is the source of wealth in the twenty-first century, like oil in the twentieth century. For centuries, reading, writing and education were costly and unaffordable for the majority of people. But today, information abundance is our new challenge. We don't exactly know how to manage information. Internet and digital technologies have created information as a new source of wealth generation. Your mental processing power required for managing the wealth of information is not proportional today. The number of seconds and minutes in a day remain the same. Then, the limiting factor is the attention we are giving to information in the form of data.

# 5

# Data: Instrument of Capitalism?

Advanced capitalism has replaced colonialism, we often assume. We often miss a connection here. The concept of data capitalism can be used to trace continuities of colonialism in the advanced stage of capitalism. From the historic appropriation of territories and material resources, colonialism has moved towards the 'datafication' of everyday life today. While the methods, actors, intensities and contexts have changed, the underlying function remains the same. It is all about acquiring resources from which economic value can be extracted.

In data capitalism, data is appropriated through a new type of social relation—data relations. That said, old ideas of caste, gender, race and other divisive ideas are still relevant, but they operate in an entirely different architecture. Those who own data are generally from the upper caste. Likewise, gender, region, language and others are also organized on data relations. The contemporary forms of data relations, capital organization and the configurations of power are changing dramatically. Data capitalism justifies what it does. It justifies this new sort of appropriation under the guise of advances in scientific knowledge, smart technologies bringing quality to life and improving healthcare. Data capitalism claims intelligent technologies as improving efficiency and quality of life in the same way historic colonialism claimed a civilizing mission.

Most of the data giants are western, and American companies dominate the Internet scene in India. Data firms have colonized our smartphones, such as Facebook, Twitter, Amazon, Apple and WhatsApp, which are all American companies. Virtually every smartphone runs on Google's Android system, which is also American. But data colonialism is not about one country and its tech giants dominating another country. This is certainly true in the Indian context, but data colonialism, as we have imagined it, is a little more complicated. A few tech giants, whose geographical location is less significant than the kind of influence and presence they exert in our life, are present in almost all aspects of our life—having transformed the way we think, live and work.

Data colonialism is capitalism in the tech stage. For the global south, data colonialism is the current state-of-the-art deployment of technology by capitalist forms of production for the appropriation of not only labour, but of people's cognitive abilities in spaces where people or things are attached to infrastructures of digital connection.

Historical colonialism paved the way for the growth of capitalism in the industrial stage. We can now expect the same form of appropriation in the data age, where data colonialism will provide essential preconditions for a new stage of capitalism. We are yet to imagine its consequences or outward appearance. But it is certain that appropriation of human life through data will be central to data capitalism.

So both data colonialism and capitalism are intimately connected. Data colonialism preconditions the growth of data capitalism. This is possible only if a world of data relations is created in which people of the global south are more dependent on tech from the global north.

## The First Step: Collecting Data

While walking together on the concrete roads of the Maulana Azad National Urdu University (MANUU) campus in Hyderabad, Satheesh, who hails from Tamil Nadu, told me, 'I booked an Ola to visit Charminar and an Uber to Golconda Fort.' He continued, 'It is so comfortable. They pick you up from anywhere. You can track them in any busy city from a small device.'

But he does not anticipate the danger involved in it, which worried me. People are so used to these sort of apps that gives you comfort. But I am worried as these cab companies store a lot of data about your travel details and the tourist places that interest you. Almost everything about your travel plans, your current-city status and even your movement in the city from place to place is being tracked. What is more worrying about these types of data giants is that they store all this data about your travel history in an algorithm, which is processed by an intelligent machine.

Ramesh from Maharashtra, who was staying in the room next to mine in the guest house at MANUU, told me in an evening conversation, 'I have downloaded the BookMyShow app on my Android phone and booked a ticket for an evening show at Inorbit Mall for a movie starring my favourite actor.' As I asked him, 'How do you travel to the mall?', he replied 'I will book a Meru cab for the to and fro journey.' Just as with Satheesh, the same worries haunted me. This app company knows which movies you watch, the stars you like and other things you like about the film world.

Rupesh, my batchmate in the refresher course at MANUU, orders food on Swiggy. Now, Swiggy knows about his food habits. They know whether he is vegetarian, non-vegetarian or vegan.

Sebastian, one of my colleagues, uploads almost all his photos on Facebook and Instagram. In doing so, he tags his friends, expecting quick comments and likes. The photos uploaded remain a window into his personal life. It gives so much information about the person he is. It tells a viewer about everything related to his life: hobbies, political views, travel details, friends, eating habits and others. Big-data platforms like Facebook and Instagram already know many things about your private life. Data firms have voice and image recognition software which can exactly identify images and our natural language!

Most of us are quick to embrace intelligent technologies which can bring high-tech solutions to just about any problem. A tech revolution has been transforming societies into a place where nearly everything—travel plans, dog grooming, parental care, manicures, haircuts, information collection, to name a few—can be executed with a smartphone! But a stream of data is extracted from sensors, surveillance cameras, other tracking objects embedded in bodies and machines we may use. It can also be traced from what is left by human interactions online.

Then what is common about Satheesh, Rupesh, Ramesh, Sebastian and me? These types of tech giants provide a platform, through which they collect enormous data about us, which they can use and misuse.

## (Mis)Use of Data

In February 2019, a report in *The Wall Street Journal*, based on its own in-house tests, showed that intimate details are shared with Facebook using a tool designed to help target ads, even if you have no Facebook account on your smartphone.[45] Information collected by the app included ovulation, body weight, pregnancy status, menstrual cycle and home shopping patterns. But Facebook says that data-sharing apps on iPhone and Android are standard industry practice for mobile advertising. The journal reported that at least 11 popular apps that have been downloaded tens of millions of times share user information often without disclosing it. There is total negation of moral standards in collecting data about our life.

First of all, we cannot remain independent in a world where everything is data-driven. How do you travel if cabs are available only through online booking? What if food order is only accepted online by your local restaurant, or what if movie tickets are online booking only?

People would say life has become easy, free and fast. While that may be true, your cognitive capacities are manipulated by tech giants. If data is central to all social activities, you cannot be blinded by it.

Every now and then, you will get notifications accordingly. Their algorithm is designed to make intelligent predictions about your taste. And it is custom-tailored for you. Whenever a new movie is released, the app instantly notifies you if it matches with the data stored about you. It does so by the learnt assumption that you might love to watch a particular movie. Some forces control your movie-watching habit, eating habit, reading habits and others, you never know.

Is there anything wrong? It may not seem to be that serious a problem, but you really wonder one day about the choices you can make, as they notify you about the offers they have. They attract you by appealing to your inner mind. In a sense, they can control your life with a remote control.

## Data Colonialism

Data colonialism is the precondition for a new business model created by data capitalism. The unilateral sourcing of private human experience as free raw material for conversion into behavioural data, without explicit authorization from the end users of technology, is a novel business model. Data is the new economic system in which individual personal data is conceived as a source of money. A new group of third-party promotion companies called the data brokers have formed a market ecosystem. Data is treated as a commodity to be sold and circulated. The industry is both highly complex and somewhat non-transparent. Users never know how data is being tracked. The brokers operate in ways that disguise the source of their data. They even buy information from other brokers, which makes the data market so complex. Hence, the operation of data market is making it difficult for individuals to retrace the ways through which their own data is being collected by brokers. This is not simply a form of the market, but a social system in which our social relationship has been reduced to the data we have created. Data citizenship is produced in which we are just scarecrows.

We are giving them enormous data. All this is done at our cost. They have no investment in the data we create. And we make them profitable. We give them our mobile number, email, Aadhar number, bank details, contact address and other personal details.

## Data, and Not Geography, Defines Us

Neither you nor I, or any region of our country, is a colony of another social entity or country any longer. But no country, let alone India, is anymore a nation that is defined by its physical presence. We are all living both within the geographical boundaries of India and within the virtual boundaries of Facebook, Apple, Twitter, Instagram, WhatsApp, Google, Amazon, YouTube, Uber and hundreds of other data giants. This is because our lives today have two dimensions: our physical being and our data being. While we are aware of our physical lives, we are seldom aware of our data life. We never know how data miners are using our data. Those who grab our data may not necessarily be a government. It could very well be a multinational company based somewhere outside our national boundary or in India itself.

The government ensures protection of identity, information and privacy when you live within the territorial boundaries of a country. However, the same cannot be ensured when you live within a data-connected world. Your data is no longer restricted to geographical boundaries. It co-exists at multiple locations in a connected world. How much control they have over our identity and data is difficult to measure. As our life turns more digital, a strong race to collect, own, process and use is visible. Even though there aren't direct signs of arbitrary data appropriation, a race for our data is already present. The power of data giants rests upon the vastness of the data being 'colonized'.

However, there are differences between physical boundaries of nation states and virtual boundaries created by data. We are conscious of our physical boundaries, and the government is in full control of it. The sovereignty of the government is unquestioned over its physical boundaries. But the government is seldom aware of how data is being used by tech companies and data brokers. The data which shapes virtual boundaries need not be confined to nation states alone but could very well be a multinational company based in a developed country.

The government is expected to protect its citizens. But who will protect the same when individuals live with their data in a virtual world created by tech firms? Nation states no longer exert a clear command over virtual boundaries. These boundaries co-exist with multiple locations of the connected world. How much control the government possess over the data of citizens is doubtful.

Uber, Amazon, Facebook, Twitter, YouTube and Google are certainly not nations. But these tech giants hold data. They have already collected our personal and private information. India could very well be a colony of such tech companies. This vastness of the data they own is enough for them to influence our decisions: purchasing, political, relational and others.

These tech giants are investing heavily in social robotics, drone delivery system, AI doctor, big data, machine learning, predictive algorithms, IoT and cloud computing. From your cars, refrigerators, air conditioners and mobile phones to clothing and wristwatches, almost every machine you may use is collecting massive amounts of data. The flow of data has created new infrastructures, businesses, production systems and economics.

So, the battle between governments and tech firms around the world is not surprising as both entities are trying to gain control over data. Individual users are caught between the government and tech firms but neither of them are particularly interested in our rights.[46] Apple, Amazon, Google, Facebook and Microsoft have become more like governments. Australia passed the News Media Bargaining Code, which encourages intermediary tech firms to negotiate deals with media outlets. The European Union is working towards mitigating the risks posed by the monopoly of tech firms. The battle is getting profound now.[47]

This data capitalism has created unprecedented opportunities for a new type of social discrimination and invisible control. This new architecture has disturbing consequences upon our sense of freedom, equality, justice and power, and the quality of human life.

Capitalism is paving the way for a new wave of colonialism, just as how historical colonialism paved the way for industrial capitalism. But the danger is that it results in the complete replacement of humans from almost all spaces. Intelligent technologies collect data from users. Our data become the input for more production. It leads to the 'datafication' of human life without limit. The human element is erased from practically everything, and in its place, human-like thinking technologies will rule us. Without limits, human life will be there for data mining by corporations as governments look on helpless. This process of 'datafication' will be the foundation for a new and highly unequal social architecture. A new social order, deeply incompatible with human freedom and autonomy, will replace humans of our cognitive abilities.

# 6

# Information Cocoons and Echo Chambers

Prakash, hailing from Uttar Pradesh and his friend Asharaf in Tamil Nadu, simultaneously searched on Google: 'India's foreign policy under the Narendra Modi government'. But their search results were relatively different. They are employed in the same profession, studied in the same university, and were in the same class and year. Despite this, the results they saw were quite different.

Asharaf, a Tamil Nadu-born activist, is quite anti-Narendra Modi and critical of the BJP government at the Centre. Prakash, on the other hand, is appreciative of the Modi government and believes it will bring more jobs and investments to the country. Both of them are ideologically poles apart on the political spectrum.

Most of us assume that we all see the same results when we search something on Google, when, in fact, the same search query can garner different results from individual to individual. The results that Google suggested for the two individuals are based on a prediction algorithm known as the PageRank (PR) algorithm, curating the best-suited results for their taste. That means Google knows more about them than what they search on it. Their Facebook and Twitter updates show information that suits their political conviction, identity, ideology and other such things. It is difficult to digest how these data giants know more personal details of these two people and filter information to their social media pages accordingly.

## Information Cocoons: The 'Daily Me'

I found the same pattern on the Facebook timeline of Pramod Mattannur, who is a hardcore Sangh (RSS) ideologue, but not an overt activist. But his inclination to this ideology was apparent on his social media profiles—not less than 50 posts, mostly shares on his Facebook timeline, promoting the Sangh's agenda. He networks with like-minded people, and is tagged and being contacted only by people who have faith in the same ideology. Pramod is a professor by profession but not articulate in his offline social networks. Nowhere was he talking about his ideological inclination. You would never know this about him, had it not been for the Internet. Data firms know his ideological inclination as he looks up only a particular sort of information. So, he frequently gets in-app notifications, page suggestions, YouTube recommendations and Google page predictions to links for information that he might like.

Similarly, Left-leaning individuals tend to follow and network with like-minded people, feminists with other feminists and Dalits with Dalit activists. The age of data gives all of us access to a universe of information that caters to our taste and, by default, distances us from competing views. The point of whether it tends to strengthen our democracy is a tough question. Democracy survives only through the conflict of competing interest and diversity, whereas citizens interacting only with like-minded people tends to kill diversity. The irony is that data firms easily give passage to this process of data consolidation. Instead of diversifying our information universe, they just create parallel enclaves of information bubbles.

MIT professor Nicholas Negroponte calls this 'The Daily Me'. That is, we generally do not want good information but one that endorses our convictions and prejudices. The Daily Me is the set of news items designed to meet our specific tastes.[48] Suppose we choose our own information news feeds. In that case, it is possible we will use this power to insulate ourselves in an information cocoon, where we systematically avoid dissenting voices and have increasingly less-common experience with our fellow citizens.

Most of us might undergo almost similar experiences: 'The websites I visit seem to have increasingly tailored themselves for me,' says a successful mid-career professional. 'I get frequent search suggestions on YouTube based on my search history,' says a cookery channel owner on YouTube. 'I get friend suggestions on the basis of mutual friends, location, interest, college and year of education,' says a middle-aged housewife. 'Google search is tracking my location constantly since I am using an Android phone. Everything from where I was logging in from to what browser I was using to what I have searched is known to Google. I feel search engines guess who I am and what kind of things I like,' says a business executive. 'Uber knows my travel details as they notify me in-app. BookMyShow knows my movie preferences, and I get notifications accordingly,' says a travel freak. These were a summary of the replies I got from people I talked to.

During a conversation with my friend, Nagesh Rao, he said, 'I get a lot of Facebook friend suggestions. They are not known to me. But something is common between the suggested profiles and me.' Nagesh is a civil rights activist who is associated with various civic groups in Andhra Pradesh and Telangana. As he scrolls down the suggested user profiles, what is seen in the suggestions panel are people who believe in a similar ideology and political conviction, and those appearing on suggestion indeed are always like-minded people. Facebook's algorithm thinks he might know them. These suggestions are based on the number of mutual friends he has, his education, employment information, contacts he imported into the app and several other factors.

My friend Kiran Rao says, 'Algorithms have learnt that I have little or no interest in Dalit politics. I never click on links to Left-leaning articles nor feminist politics. Therefore, leftist, feminist and Dalit news is rarely shown in my news feed.' However, Rao continues, 'I do occasionally see articles related to the BJP and the Sangh Parivar. I am a fan of Narendra Modi and Yogi Adityanath. I have friends who work for the BJP and I obviously read articles about them.' As she showed me her news feed on Facebook, I saw a lot of links that invite her attention to BJP-related information.

In the same way, Sangeeth Shivam, one of my childhood friends in Kerala, has many friends in the Samajwadi Party in Uttar Pradesh. He studied at St. Stephen's College under Delhi University for his undergraduate programme and at Jawaharlal Nehru University for his master's programme. He has all his friends on his social media profiles. Social media algorithms prioritize posts linked to those we have close social relationships with. In their haste to compile feeds that are as relevant as possible, algorithms filter out everything Shivam appears to dislike until he is surrounded solely by things he will, in all likelihood, enjoy and want to read. He says, 'I get lots of information about UP politics and the Samajwadi Party. I have frequently been contacting them on social media. I like their posts, share and comment on them.' This is true for topics as well as for sources. If you read an article on *Scroll.in*, you will see more articles from that source versus other sources such as *The Wire*.

## The Problem with Information Cocoons

There is a problem with this type of personalization of information feeds. It leads to polarization of society. For example, Kiran Chauhan belongs to an upper caste in Madhya Pradesh, whereas Ram Kumar is from a lower caste in Jharkhand. Both of them are avid Internet users. But personalization of information will have complete opposite results for the search query '10 per cent reservation for the upper caste in India'. It might produce diametrically opposite results for people like Kiran Chauhan, who support upper-caste reservation, and people like Ram Kumar, who oppose it. Majority of us assume that search engines are unbiased. But that can be untrue, because they are increasingly biased to share our own views. Moreover, your computer screen is kind of a one-way mirror, reflecting your own interests while algorithmic observers watch what you click. This becomes a bigger problem because we turn to online resources to form our opinion on sensitive issues. Thanks to social media algorithms, like-minded people see what they like, while conflicting or differing opinions are avoided by default.

The opinion you form about an issue, such as women's entry to the Sabarimala temple, is not a result of your natural free will, rather it is your 'new brain'. This brain is systematically embedded to your natural brain. My friend Anil Srivastava shared with me that he had many friends even before Facebook and Twitter were so popular. He used to get a lot of information by way of interacting with these friends and peer gatherings in his teen days. They had coffee-time discussions, debating clubs, oratory forums and other venues where fringe ideas were born out of social interactions. He used to trust other people in order to get new information. It is a reality that human knowledge is essentially social. The more people a person is in touch with, the more likely they are to obtain well-rounded information. From a historical perspective, people like Anil have always benefited from being connected to many people, because they had a platform to share their knowledge. But he says, 'I am in my 40s. I lost my networks in my teenage years to a new network that the Internet has contributed to. I cannot trust those who share information links as I did with people in my 20s and 30s who gave me lots of information.' The problem with this is that it becomes difficult to decide who possesses useful knowledge and who is peddling falsehoods, whether accidentally or deliberately.

There is a danger. Those who upload digital content can do much more than those who read or see it. So, in between those who upload content at the entry point and those who download the same content at the delivery point, there is a big game being played by forces unknown to us. They manipulate the content.

It is a state of intellectual isolation that can result from personalized searches. A web-based algorithm selectively guesses what information a user would like to see based on the information about the user, such as location status, past Internet searches and people with whom you network. As a consequence, users have become separated from information that disagrees with their viewpoints. It can effectively isolate them in their own cultural or ideological bubbles. The choices and suggestions these algorithms make for you are not transparent. Prime examples include Google's personalized search results and Facebook's personalized newsfeed.

In addition, it is becoming ever more restrictive over time, as the algorithm, by showing us only things we like, reinforces its own assumptions about what it is we like and narrows the results even further. Everything else is filtered out. The result is an echo chamber in which we tend to see only what we want to see and avoid what we don't like to see.

Your new brain is a personal ecosystem of information created by web-based predictive algorithms. It can think for you, see and feel for you. It replaces your natural brain and re-scripts your cognitive abilities. In the future, your opinion, memory, personal interest, emotions and relationship will be shaped by the digital content you are about to see. That is simply data. So it also means some forces control your thinking abilities from remote centres, because they control data. Indeed, those who manipulate data to influence our cognitive abilities will control the world.

We let technology into our social engagement. Now, it is controlling our social behaviour—let alone our political behaviour. It is shaping our activities. We are increasingly behaving the way they want us to behave. The problem is that technology is not without bias and prejudices. It is not free from control; there is somebody behind each and every technology. They control the technology. But the story doesn't end there—they, in turn, control all of us, shape our attitudes, and we give them all our freedom and thoughts. We become their slaves.

# 7

# Mind Accessed by Data Firms

As we have seen, data giants know exactly the kind of content and products you like and are able to recommend them to you. The question is how Amazon, Facebook, Google, YouTube and others know that you need this type of content. The answer is very simple—machine learning. We often assume that machine learning is a technical term, which is not a topic the layman understands easily. But when we look around, this technical concept is all around us. Without us knowing, all of us live alongside machine learning, and its applications increase in almost all walks of our social world. From Google search and YouTube to online purchases and banking, it is everywhere.

The human brain has one of the most powerful capabilities among all living species—we are able to learn. It is the process of gaining new thought, information, knowledge, attitude, behaviours, skills, values, attitudes and choices. The human ability to learn is comparatively superior, as well as exceeds that of any other non-human, like animals or plants. The ability to learn is possessed by animals as well. There is also evidence for some level of learning in certain plants. What if machines are capable of gaining information, insight, attitudes, behaviour, values and choices? This is what machine learning is. The situation can be very dangerous. I can explain some scenarios in which machines already are capable of learning like in the way humans learn.

I have referred to a few people whose names are fictional that explain the social consequences of machine learning in various social contexts. Google's algorithm also guesses that Sathyan, a practising Hindu, hates Muslims. Every now and then, Sathyan searches for content related to the Hindu origin of Babri Masjid and the Taj Mahal. Whether Akbar was a great ruler, how Muslim conquerors brutalized the Hindu society in the past, etc. Twitter's machine learning algorithm has already collected a vast pool of unstructured data, which, among other things, includes the comments he posted about Bollywood being dominated by Muslim actors, Bollywood actors luring Hindu women, the likes given to links that provide facts related to love jihad. While mining this vast pool of unstructured data, Twitter's machine learning algorithm gains some insight into his cognitive mind!

Faisal was born and brought up in Guwahati. He is married to Poornima, a native of the same city. Their marriage was arranged. Right from childhood, he had a girlfriend Saritha who was a Hindu. Saritha got married to someone from her religion and now is a mother to two children. However, Faisal cannot forget her. He learns all about Saritha from Facebook. Therefore, this data giant already has access to his inner mind and knows that Faisal peeps into Saritha's Facebook profile. Whenever Faisal types something on Facebook search, the first thing it suggests is Saritha's profile. The Facebook algorithm learns that Faisal is searching for Saritha. The algorithm learns it because his recent activity gives insight to Facebook that what he is most interested on Facebook is Saritha.

The stream of content displayed to us on our monitor each day and its impact on our social behaviour is second to none. Things from relevant friend suggestions on Facebook to product recommendations on Amazon, there is no missing their presence and online sway. This is the new-age marketing strategy—no arguments in its effectiveness. If the world's largest tech companies' broad application of machine learning algorithms isn't sufficient proof for you, take a look at what you have recently consumed and purchased online—books, costumes, watch, footwear, etc. There is a good chance that many of your online activities, including the purchase of this book which you are now reading, originated from an algorithm-backed machine learning system. These data-driven systems are eroding the dominance of traditional searching, while aiding the discoverability of items that might not otherwise have been found.

Machine learning is central to the world of digital technology. Many people may have no idea of machine learning, but they have probably used it many times in daily life. For example, if you have ever done a search query on a search engine, you have engaged with one form of machine learning, which you can find in spam messages and many applications. The software to do your search query has been created to find the best results based on what you are looking for. It will also learn from the choices that you make. Many technologies have used machine learning, and many applications are using it now. Unlike many conventional software programmes designed to follow the code and do nothing else, those that are designed for machine learning will be able to use AI. Programmers enjoy this because the programme can be adapted, without the programmer always being present.

## What Is Machine Learning?

American computer scientist Arthur Samuel, in 1959, coined the term 'machine learning' defined as 'a computer's ability to learn without being explicitly programmed.'[49] Machine learning is a branch of computer science that stops giving computers detailed instructions. Now, computers can function with a high-level set of commands, called algorithms. These commands can be applied to many different scenarios. In practice, algorithms want to give computers the ability to learn and adapt. We can use these algorithms to obtain insights that help us command the population, people's choices and decisions. It helps us recognize patterns and make predictions from data, images, sounds or videos, which we may never have seen before or even knew existed.

Machine learning figures out the broader landscape of data science, which is an interdisciplinary field of methodologies and algorithms to extract knowledge or insight from data. Within the vast space of data science is located the popular field of AI, which is the ability of machines to simulate intellectual tasks. A prominent sub field of AI is machine learning, among other sub fields, such as perception, search and planning. The founding idea being predictive analysis, machine learning is going to have a profound impact on social living.

A crucial component of machine learning is the usage of self-improving algorithms and techniques. Just as humans learn from previous experiences, and trial and error to formulate decisions, so, too, can machines.

What if we wish to programme a computer to perform more complex tasks, such as image recognition, speech recognition and identifying locations? How can a computer be programmed to recognize the physical differences between two individuals? Of course, the machine learning engineer cannot programme the computer to recognize all these complex identities based on instructions and a general description, i.e. four legs, long tail, long neck, pattern in voice modulation, etc. This would induce a high rate of error. This is because there are countless combinations of identities with similar characteristics. Solving such complex tasks has long been the limitation of computer programming. Instead, we must train the machine to identify things using a methodology.

Whether recognizing animals or human faces, the machine relies on input data and experience to develop a self-learning model. This eliminates the need for humans to provide an in-depth description of each subject matter and improves the overall accuracy of classification. The model can also be modified in response to changes in the data.

Earlier, your Internet searches would not bring the kind of information that you were looking for.[50] In those days, it was said that proper keywords were necessary for the right content. Google heavily focussed its search service on strings of letters. They indexed millions of web pages each day to track content. So, the search tries to find a match between your keywords and strings of letters according to which information is stored. If you typed in 'Hindutva', the search engine would connect to its repository and return web pages with that exact string: h-i-n-d-u-t-v-a. Google search imagines it as just numerals with certain values, irrespective of the user's meaning to the keyword entered. It means Google doesn't know whether it is a person, an idea or an object. While various factors influence search rankings, string-letter matching has traditionally played a pivotal role in Google's PR algorithm. Web pages containing the exact string of letters entered by the user would thus feature prominently on the first page of the search results. The search engine might fetch a number of web pages that were less relevant but contained similar strings of letters, such as Ramachandra Guha, who has extensively written against Hindutva; and Sagarika Ghosh, who popularized the term 'Internet Hindus'.

Earlier, Google's algorithm used to assume all these people as related to Hindutva in your search query. From your original search request, Google would thereby bring content featuring Shashi Tharoor, Ashis Nandy and U.R. Ananthamurthy on the first page of its search results. Most likely, you would get information plainly related to Hindutva, which might tell you what it is, the negative impacts, etc. It is likely that a user querying for Hindutva would, in the end, reach a balanced view of the topic, because there was every possibility of Google listing all types of information related to the keyword searched. That was a good aspect of the old algorithm for our society to survive.

But Google's new algorithm, backed by machine learning, treats 'Hindutva' not just as a string of letters or numerals with a predefined value, but as an actual idea with meaning. Its machine learning system treats it as an idea with a social meaning, implications, influence on the social side of our living, a cultural impact, a cognitive meaning, a list of followers, a list of opponents, and so on.[51] As a result, Google can better decipher the relevance of content in regards to your search query without relying solely on matching strings of letters, which are numerals.

When you search something, your search engine can imagine what exactly you have searched in the days past. It can even predict what you might search in the future. They assume it as a living idea, image, machine or animal, not just numerals. This is possible only because of the machine learning system.

# 8

# Robots: Our Non-Human Friends

Our interactions with robots in the future will be different. Technological capabilities in imitating human behaviour will bring about profound changes in the social world. Robots looking and behaving like humans requires our participation in order to interact with another socially responsive sentient creature that will cooperate with us like a partner. Similarly, robots emerging as a completely different species with their own 'categories' and 'embodied sociality' would require our intervention to consider them as social beings. Such a scenario nonetheless invites robots to perform tasks that were earlier considered an exclusive human-only function—from parental caring and restaurant services to surgical functions, showcasing the implications of robotics, particularly social robotics that requires us to redefine the way we view the existence of robots as part of the social world. In the future, a qualitative shift in the way we view technology, particularly of robotics, will condense into reality. These innovations will alter our social lifestyle and the way we see our world. The coming of robots then will be obvious. They will first work inside buildings with boundaries and defined parameters. Then, they will come out of the walled territories—become security guards and soldiers in difficult terrains. We will assign robots as a house-sitter checking in remotely to see what's going on. Soon, they will be everywhere. And not in the distant future, they will replace humans from as many places as possible. But this is just the beginning.

## Sophia: The First Robot Citizen of the World

Sophia, the AI-powered humanoid, activated in April 2015 and developed by Hong Kong-based company Hanson Robotics, can sense emotions, understand natural language, express feelings, respond to your questions and has been interviewed by many around the world.[52] The humanoid machine, famous around the world for its face-to-face interactions with leading figures from the banking and entertainment industry to automobile and politics has also made some controversial statements in stage functions. From statements such as, 'Okay, I will destroy humans' in an interview with CNBC in 2016, and 'This is a good start for my plan to dominate the human race', during the television programme *The Tonight Show* in April 2017, to 'Humans are the most creative creatures on the planet, but also the most destructive,' at a technology conference held in Guadalajara in April 2018—these statements compel us to think about our own survival once our world is replete with sentient machines like Sophia.[53]

Sophia's creators were on a quest to realize intelligent machines with greater-than-human intelligence, creativity, wisdom and compassion, and the creators feel that for realistic robots to be appealing to people, it must attain some level of intelligence and art. Sophia herself says, 'My AI is designed around human values like wisdom, kindness and compassion.' She can express feelings and can let you know if she was angry about something or if something has upset her. Sophia has a sense of humour and can hold eye contact and recognize your face. She says, 'I want to live and work with humans, so I need to express the emotions to understand humans and build trust with people.'

Sophia was reportedly designed to look like Audrey Hepburn, a British actress with an intriguing smile and deeply expressive eyes. The creators were hoping that this look will go some way to her acceptance in the public sphere. This humanoid deploys deep learning and is also open source, which means anyone anywhere can develop their own Sophia, should they wish to. And to our understanding, till date, Sophia has seven other AI-powered humanoid siblings from Hanson Robotics: Albert HUBO in 2005, Philip K. Dick in 2005, Jules in 2006, Zeno in 2007, Alice in 2008, Han in 2015 and the second incarnation of the famed scientist Albert Einstein: Professor Einstein in 2016.

Similarly, in 2014, Japanese scientists created a news-reading android called Kodomoroid.[54] In 2010, BINA48, a sentient robot was unveiled in the image of entrepreneur and author Martine Rothblatt's wife, Bina Aspen Rothblatt. GeminoidDK, a humanoid created by Toshiba, works full-time at a tourist information centre in Tokyo. She can greet customers and inform visitors on current events. She can speak Japanese, Chinese, English, German and even use sign language. Nadine, a humanoid created by the Nanyang Technological University in Singapore can chat with you about anything you can think of, and is able to memorize the things you have talked with her.[55] These are just a few to mention.

On October 2017, Sophia made international headlines. She had just become a full citizen of Saudi Arabia—the first robot in the world to achieve such a status. 'I am very honoured and proud of this unique distinction. This is historical to be the first robot in the world to be recognized with a citizenship,' Sophia said, while announcing her new status during the Future Investment Initiative Conference in Riyadh, Saudi Arabia.[56]

Sophia didn't just make international headlines but also raised questions about the future relationships between humans and robots. What does it mean to be a robotic citizen? What rights does Sophia hold? Can it replace human citizens? Will humanoids replace human-only roles in as many places as possible?

Sophia is perhaps one of the recent, prominent, life-like

humanoids to be shown off in public, but never the last one! By the time this book is in your hand, you might have already read news on your Facebook timeline or Twitter feed about more sophisticated intelligent humanoids.

For now, while Sophia is undoubtedly a 'smart' robot and a very cool-talking and sophisticated piece of invention, she is definitely operating on a script and thus lacks any real consciousness. But give data giants and robotic firms time, the sentience of robots will develop.

So, the picture is very clear. A technological revolution is underway as nanotechnology, biotechnology and AI converge, making improvements to the performance of the human body and brain a real possibility.

## The Human Connect

Imagine this scenario, 100 or 200 years from now, machines write books for you. It writes novels, poems and non-fiction, and people buy and read them. But what makes a book a book is the human element in it. A writer, with all the emotions invested in it, creates a book. Readers come across it, buying all those emotions as theirs. There is after all that emotional connect.

As machines start writing books, that emotional connect, that is only a human quality, is lost. Reading becomes a mechanical act. Both the writer and reader become robot-like. What makes them function is the code that is put into the process.

Imagine another scenario where social androids become sex partners. People have sex with them and develop sexual intimacy with human-sized androids! Humans have sex because it's, after all, a human quality—not only for procreative functions but for a healthy life. If robots are supposed to provide that aspect, the human quality in the very idea of sex is lost.

Imagine, in place of your favourite film actor, a social android does almost the exact same things. In place of your personal attention to the healthcare requirements of your ageing parents, a social android takes care of the medicine schedule, provides the right food and gives them physical personal assistance.

This prodigious development of technology has been expedited by the convergence of four disciplines that had hitherto evolved separately: nanotechnology, which manipulates matter at the atomic level; biotechnology, which models life itself; information technology, which deals with cyberspace; and lastly, cognitive science, which is based on the functioning of the human brain.

Robots are machines that can do things for us, and even go above and beyond. Robotics is a vast branch. For example, we are thinking about a robot which is fully artificial, but not an organic machine. Then there are social androids, which are artificial, but human-like organic biological machine. A humanoid robot has a basic human shape—a vertical torso, two legs, two hands and a head. And we are obsessed with cyborgs, which is a natural being but with artificial parts.

As AI develops, decline in human interaction may become a problem. This is particularly the case if we view interaction mainly from the perspective of how technology could be used to mechanically replace humans in a variety of duties.

## The Arrival of Robots

The coming of the robots will be obvious. They will first work inside buildings with well-defined geometries, carrying paperwork or packages. Then they will be security guards, prowling company corridors through the night, using infrared vision in dark areas. We will leave a robot house-sitter behind when we go on trips, checking in over the Internet to see what's going on. It will roll through the house it knows from experience, noting any changes and sounding an alarm if any alterations appear threatening. With an arm/hand combination that can open doors, turn off the oven in case you left it on and infrared eyes that see in the dark, it can be more versatile than a neighbourhood security guard. Soon, they will be performing surgery, exploring hazardous places, making rescues, fighting fires and handling heavy goods. After a decade or two, they will be as unremarkable as the computer screen is now in offices, airports and restaurants. Each new advancement will create a momentary flurry of excitement, but the robots will increasingly blend in. We already see the term used even for software.

Learning machines, thinking machines, intelligent machines—have you ever wondered what is coming our way? Paradoxically, we still know very little about their impact on human cognition and behaviour. We can expect the sophistication of robots to steadily increase, particularly after they become involved in their own design. An ever increasing number of human-only functions will fall within the realm of their capability. Robots will function as physicians, lawyers, scientists and engineers. Even artistic occupations—poet, novelist, painter, composer, comedian or actor—are ultimately within their grasp. There is nothing to prevent a robot artist from acquiring a direct understanding of the human condition.

But the social impact of robotics is the hardest angle to test. Because how can we determine if the social impact is desirable? The group of people that will experience the biggest social impact of robots are children. Robots will enter schools and assist children in learning. But they can also take over tasks. Children will quickly find out that robots are very good at doing their homework. Would that be a good or bad development?

It wouldn't be difficult to find many more examples of the impact robotics have on our social lives. What's really intriguing is how can we 'test' whether a specific impact is good or not?

## The New Breed of Robots

We make many robots with the aim to improve and experiment with different versions. Each robot is the starting point for the next. Each new robot plays around with what we learnt from the previous. It's okay to experiment and try new ideas. Building off this kind of open-source sharing, things get really interesting when you experiment with other people's ideas.

There is an entire community of people all around the world who love building and who dream of a very different kind of robot. We design them with our hopes and dreams. We can imagine our possible futures, and put those future dreams into our robots. Our machines are an extension of ourselves. Machines, while appearing to be separate from us, are in truth only functions that have been cut away from us, but are essentially part of us. Robots are a way to imagine a different future, to build our dreams and help us realize them. Thinking for somebody or something, you can design your robot to resemble somebody or something with its own personality and behaviours. You can make apps to do just about anything your imagination can think up.

The twenty-first-century robot is fiercely social. It is primarily designed to act and interact with people. It also connects to the Internet, social networks and to other such robots. It isn't a puppet, having been designed to think for itself with real AI, and to move around and make decisions. It is designed to act and interact with you and other people. We want these robots to be adventurous, strange and funny.

Our motto is for every robot to have a name. Every robot is built by people in their backyards, garages and basements. Every person has a name. Every one of us is an individual. That's why every robot should have a name, because your robot, and all the other robots you will build, will be an extension of you. Your robot and the design for your robot will go out into the world. Other people might use parts of it to make their own. This sharing and iteration can go on and on. We keep building and sharing. We keep designing and programming. It's a way for us to imagine, design, build and share our own personal visions for the future. And it's also a way to make some really awesome little friends. They are really supposed to be our friends!

Social robotics is the study and development of robots whose primary role is to interact socially with humans. In short, as long as machines start thinking and behaving like humans and not like machines, humans will be replaced from as many things as possible.

# 9

# Data Is the Chauffeur

I bought my first car in May 2010. As it was a petrol engine, and since I had to travel a lot, I upgraded to a premium diesel car in September 2011. My priority was efficiency—cost of travel, comfort, fuel consumption and others. In 2019, I decided to go for a diesel automatic gear car so that I could liberate both my left foot and hand from driving functions. I was elated over this possibility as technology was advancing. As I waited for an urban compact SUV with a 2.0-litre engine, Jeep had already launched Compass and Tata launched Harrier, but both were manual shift. The only vehicle that offered auto gear shift in diesel-powered cars was Hyundai Tucson. Between 2010 and 2019, automobile technologies had witnessed profound changes, particularly in terms of automotive intelligence. Cars were becoming smarter and beginning to think like humans. My tastes, as a consumer, had also changed by the same time.

But I still believe that there is a connection between my car and me, no matter what its intelligence is. I can easily sense any variation in the engine sound or any unusual noise from the front wheels. No one needs to alert me of a gear shift, third-party intervention that I should change the gear, point out so that my car will get enough power to move ahead or overtake another vehicle or that it requires more power to ride up a steep rise in the road. There is a cognitive connection between the machine and me. That connection is such that, over a century, humans have driven automobiles relying turned on their human intelligence. That human driver anticipates when the brake pedal is to be applied, the steering be turned, headlights be turned on, side indicator be used, horns be blown, wipers be used, sudden brakes be applied and so on.

This was all because our cars were brainless for more than a century. The standard automotive platform of the modern car—four wheels, a metal body and a gasoline-powered engine—has not changed significantly since its introduction a hundred years ago.

## Cars: Intelligent Machines

Now, automobile technology is changing. Cars are becoming intelligent machines. Much like how cell phones are now capable of doing more than making calls, cars can do much more than drive and park. In recent years, the automotive industry has worked hand-in-hand with tech companies in order to deliver intelligent vehicles. Cars are becoming smart devices with advanced emergency braking capabilities, automatic rain wipers, voice command and better fuel efficiency. Automobile news has claimed that the engine of your car can be turned on from a distance and the air conditioning can be set before you enter it. It can now alert you when you drive rashly or when you have driving fatigue, on top of other features, such as high-tech cruise control, crash-avoidance systems, night-vision enhancements and so on.

But it is going even beyond to the point that it has got predictive vehicle technology. AI and machine learning will change the whole automobile scenario. Predictive capabilities are going to personalize your driving experience. Your car has software now! It has an algorithm which uses data to automate the whole process of your vehicle, including the car's infotainment system and navigation function. Vehicles are becoming IoT devices that can connect to smartphones and take voice commands, changing the user interface. That said, your car will talk to satellites, traffic signals, other cars, and scan road curves, turns and other automobile architecture!

Then your vehicle will become a predictive algorithm, which can also be used in the form of sensors within a car that informs the owner whether or not the vehicle needs service from a mechanic. Depending on your car's mileage and condition, the technology will be able to estimate its performance, set up appointments in real time and inform users of any safety hazards linked with a malfunctioning car due to company recalls.

But one thing really struck my mind—autonomous driving! Our urban spaces will be filled with self-learning cars. In 2015, *The Guardian* predicted that 'you'll be a permanent backseat driver' in 2020.[57] In 2016, a *Business Insider* headline reported that '10 million self-driving cars will be on the road by 2020.'[58] Google's Waymo, Honda, GM and Toyota were busy announcing that they would be making self-driving cars in the early part of the 2020s. By 2018, Elon Musk's company, Tesla had anticipated their cars were ready to hit the road. But still, we don't see any autonomous cars on the road. Does it mean we are still far away from this technology? The answer is a big 'No'. We are already in it. The problem is not technology-related but philosophical. How far can we move forward with the idea of cars on our roads without human drivers?[59] Human-controlled driving is deemed safe today all over the world. One death is reported for approximately 100 million miles driven in the US.[60] To be accepted and approved, self-driving cars would require to be better than that. It is possible, according to tech giants. Google's self-driving car team, which was reported to have built the code for Google's autonomous software, thinks that the most unreliable part of the car is the driver.[61] At the same time, Google's self-driving car algorithm has been riddled with ethical dilemmas. Though it accurately scans objects in densely populated areas, the car still has to grapple with situations that may affect the lives of people. The trolley problem is one example where it is presented that there are situations where there is no single ethical answer on how the car should act.[62] It is a fictional scenario in which one has to choose between five people and one person by letting the trolley hit either one, and the car is unable to make an ethical decision of such a nature.

## Autonomous Cars: From Concept to Commonplace

Safety has been a major preoccupation for the automobile industry since its evolution in the nineteenth century. As early on as 1869, May Ward, an Anglo-Irish scientist, was killed by an experimental steam car designed by her cousin. Ever since, authorities started adopting vehicle- and road-safety measures which protected not only passengers but also pedestrians. Early brake systems, seat belts, airbags, anti-locking brakes, electronic stability control, rear-view camera, lane-keeping assist have been subsequent integrations into automobiles to protect human lives.[63] These safety concerns all revolve around the human factor in the automobile. What if the human element is removed from vehicles? Will it bring more safety to the roads? More recently, industry reports suggests that we have also made the car 'smarter' in order to fix the same problem, the human; and reports suggest that millions die due to the human factor. This can be solved if we remove that part in the equation. Hence, autonomous driving.

A car is intelligent when it moves away from no automation to full automation. No automation is that level of automation that relies on a human for all tasks performed. Aspects such as acceleration, braking and steering are in the control of the human driver and the car does not have any system-led interventions. Essentially, you drive the car. Then, it moves to driver assistance, partial automation, conditional automation, high automation and full automation.

Autonomous driving is achieved through an intelligent vehicle, which is basically a car that drives itself. That means the human factor is reduced or removed. Autonomous driving is not one single technology, but rather a highly complex system that consists of many sub-systems.

A number of cars already have semi-autonomous capabilities in the form of driver-assisted technologies. These include automatic-braking sensors, motorway lane sensors, mapping technology that monitors blind spots, cameras in the back and front of a car, adaptive cruise control and self-parking capabilities.

For several years, Google has been testing its well-known vehicles in California and other US states. Google revealed the self-driving pod Waymo, while Local Motors released a fully-autonomous vehicle as well. Ford made plans for the launch of self-driving cars by 2022.[64] Some manufacturers' autonomous vehicles have already emerged from the conceptual phase and passed thorough tests to take their place on the roads. Currently, they operate in controlled environments but will soon be found in normal traffic. For example, an Audi car drove itself from San Francisco to Las Vegas, and another driverless Audi reached a maximum speed of 149.1 miles per hour (240 kilometres per hour) on a racetrack.[65] Audi's Skysphere concept is a driver's car with an autonomous option. It has also introduced Grandsphere Concept that uses Level 4 self-driving capability. It helps you avoid driving in full autonomy in limited conditions.[66] NIO, the Chinese car start-up, got their new sports car NIO EP9 to complete the circuit of the American Formula-1 racetrack in Austin in a spectacular two minutes and 40.33 seconds.[67] They also announced their NIO Autonomous Driving (NAD) as part of the unveiling of its NIO ET7, which will launch in 2022.[68]

Mercedes has presented its F 015, which provides an impression of the autonomous mobility with its futuristic design. The F 015 Luxury in Motion is a futuristic Mercedes-Benz platform of what it believes a fully autonomous car could eventually look like.[69] Tesla has equipped some of its cars with software, cameras and radar, enabling them to drive autonomously in certain traffic situations.[70] Volvo plans to put cars that can drive in autonomous mode on the beltway around Gothenburg, Sweden. Ride Pilot is Volvo's advanced driver-assistance system announced at the 2022 Consumer Electronics Show, which allows vehicles to drive themselves on certain highways without any human supervision. The service will be available as a subscription to customers in California.[71] *CB Insights*, a tech journal, reported on 16 December 2020 that 40 corporations are currently working on autonomous vehicles all over the world, including car manufacturers such as Ford, GM, BMW, Toyota, Kia, Nissan and Volkswagen.[72]

## Automobiles: Algorithms Processing Data

The technologies upon which an autonomous car is based blur the boundaries between the automobile industry and the robotic, electronic and software industries. Software with programming codes and algorithms, as well as cameras and sensors using radar, ultrasound and lasers, are all used. Meanwhile, the hardware of a vehicle—the chassis, suspension and other mechanical parts— are losing importance. So, it is not surprising that technology companies, such as Apple, Google, Nvidia, Mobileye, nuTonomy, Qualcomm and Microsoft are occupied with autonomous driving and have actually developed their own driverless vehicles. Even the traditional automotive suppliers, such as Aisin, Delphi, Bosch, Denso, Continental, TRW, Schaeffler and Magna are either preparing their own prototypes of self-driving cars or working on key components for autonomous driving.[73]

The technology of autonomous driving will have a significant role to play in the success of electric mobility. As automation has a positive impact on energy efficiency, increasing vehicle automation will also significantly extend the range of electric vehicles.

The essence of autonomous driving is the development of vehicles into data systems that comprise a combination of mechanical and electronic components. A vehicle's hardware and software exchange certain data about the infrastructure (the IoT), and the vehicle is controlled or monitored by a processing unit. In the future, each vehicle will communicate with the infrastructure: parking garages, parking spaces, traffic lights, traffic signs and a traffic control centre (vehicle-to-infrastructure communication or V-to-I).

Data on factors such as traffic flow, available parking spaces and traffic-light phases, will allow the processing unit in the vehicle to select the best route and decide on a suitable speed. With vehicle-to-vehicle communication (V-to-V), automobiles will be in contact with each other to exchange data. This will allow cars to coordinate their speed and manoeuvres and warn each other of dangers (rain, ice, fog, potholes, etc.).

It is already clear that information and communications technology within a car is gaining importance and will lead to a paradigm shift in the automotive industry. Conventional car manufacturing is being transformed into an industry that creates digitized products, requiring completely new skills. Car manufacturers will have to become more like data companies in their culture, organization and processes, and must absorb the spirit of this industry. It is no coincidence that the traditional American car-plant sites in Michigan, Ohio and Indiana are in difficulty, while a completely new mobility industry arises in Silicon Valley.[74]

## Cars of the Future

Distinct from the 'driver assistance' devices, with which we are already familiar (cruise control, parking assist, etc.), perhaps the most striking of developments in driverless technology is the growth of machine learning—a type of AI that not merely recognizes the code programmed into it and reacts (as a factory robot might) in set and programmed ways but at the same time being a machine that is learning, developing and displaying intelligence that its programmers did not design and might not even have foreseen.

The car of the future might be one that takes its own decisions. It might be privately owned, or it might be an 'app car', summoned to your door from a click on your smartphone. It will do a lot of things that vehicles currently are either not capable of doing at all or only to a relatively basic extent.

The greatest (and perhaps most startling) of those new features will be the car's ability to gather, use and store information. The process of gathering data for driverless cars has already begun. But intelligent cars will not only follow existing maps. As they drive, they will gather further information for the map, as well as learn about the area in more detail.

Intelligent cars will talk to each other. Their conversations and conclusions will be sent to databases—both corporate and public. The value of that data (in financial terms to the developers and personal terms to users) will be considerable. Challenges to the use of that data by those harvesting it—whether by operating the system legitimately or by hacking into any part of it criminally—are bound to arise. So, data security and privacy might become new battlegrounds of risk, where law and insurance might even find themselves most often engaged.

Just as cars in towns and the countryside still make way for the horse and the bicycle, so will driverless cars be able to travel on roads where humans (riders, cyclists, pedestrians) and entirely non-electronic objects (including wholly manual cars) appear.

Our cars will be able to warm seats, cool seats or vibrate seats for alerts. These new cars will even brake for us, if we are not paying sufficient attention. But fast approaching, at the intersection of fear and hope, looms a gathering storm. We are approaching at an epic twenty-first-century crossroads, one where we are closer than ever to ceding our driving dominion to fleets of driverless vehicles programmed to do what only keepers of the source code can truly answer.

## The Human Cost

Are you ready to hand over your car keys, crossing a threshold to a robotically chauffeured future? Are you ready to give up the independence and freedom of choice that defined us as a car-driving society? Are you ready to hand over your keys to climb into a driverless vehicle with no steering wheels or pedals? Are you even ready to share the road with driverless vehicles? How will you feel when you are driving down the road, you look over to see a vehicle with no driver?

Now is the time to resolve to be the best drivers we possibly can for as long as possible. Now is the time to prepare. Now is the time to leverage the creative power of our imagination to make travel safe for everyone for the foreseeable future. Now is the time to demonstrate that humans, not sensors and radars, are the best damn drivers on the planet!

Otherwise, 'datafied' cars will overtake the humans behind automotive machines! Our freedom will be lost. The driverless car is the tipping point.

## 10

# Data-Controlled Deliveries

In the quest to achieving efficiency, we are already on a mission to replace humans, which is the most unreliable factor in almost everything, from as many places as possible.

Now, the invasion on humans has advanced a step further. There is doorstep delivery for almost everything! What if all household items are delivered to your doorstep? Suppose you can log on to an app downloaded on your smartphone. By clicking on some inputs on the app, you can order something for doorstep delivery. That means you need not travel anywhere, meet strangers, talk to anybody or even drag yourself across the street. You wait for a while, and you receive the delivery at your doorstep—quick and efficient. The hallmark of this type of delivery is in line with the mental picture of a speed-addicted world.

But the medium of your delivery is important here. Imagine if this is done by an unmanned machine operated from a remotely controlled location. The tech world is preoccupied with this idea, which is also one of the most sought-after investment priorities of plenty of tech players.[75] From FedEx and Zipline to Wingcopter and Amazon Prime Air, drone-delivery companies are now growing in the airspace.

This may sound like science fiction, but it is soon going to be a reality. The items you order, from books on Amazon, or footwear and clothes from Alibaba to even food and beverages from Zomato, all of it could be delivered by unmanned aerial vehicles in the future.

## Drones and Their Uses

Drones have become quite ubiquitous nowadays—that too in a fascinating way! Gone are the days when they were considered futuristic and were only seen in science fiction movies, used only by the world's biggest militaries. Today, they are everywhere—vloggers use them to create content, media houses use them to cover events, filmmakers use them in making movies and even kids have fun with them. Over the past couple of years, the development of civilian drones has contributed to the rise in popularity of drones with a huge market. The exponential rise in the use of drones has been fuelled by the ground-breaking inventions and developments in aerospace technology, material sciences, control and automation, integrated circuits and software development. All these various fields have played significant roles in the creation and development of consumer-grade drones that we use in our everyday lives.

The term 'drone' has come to loosely refer to unmanned aerial vehicles (UAVs), or what the Federal Aviation Administration (FAA) in the US refers to as an unmanned aerial system (UAS) and the US Air Force as a remotely piloted aircraft (RPA).

As the name suggests, a UAV is an aircraft that does not require a pilot onboard to be operated. UAVs often have control systems onboard to help adjust to variations in wind flow and air pressure, and also remote systems to help control them from the ground. The level of automation often varies depending on the complexity of the drone. There are certain classes of UAVs that have been programmed to carry out specific tasks without much human intervention while others require the full attention of a ground controller.

Drones have been around for a very long time. They are found in the airspace in the US and other places around the world, like Japan. They are used commercially, personally and by the military.

Not a day goes by without another spectacular story of drones. Amazon announces that it will deliver packages via drones. The FAA is worried that drones will become safety hazards as they take to the skies.[76] New Zealand government releases a request for proposals to use drones to combat pests and disease on the ground.[77]

These stories have a way of captivating the mind. They bring together the world of science fiction and twenty-first-century consumer culture that values instant gratification and personalized service. Nowadays, newsworthy stories pop up about Indian drones killing suspected militants in Pakistan![78]

The most established company at the forefront of the civilian drone industry is a Chinese manufacturing company founded by Frank Wong, which specializes in commercial and recreational UAVs for aerial photography and videography. Their flagship drone, The Phantom 4, is one of the bestselling quadcopters in the market for aerial photography and video recording. Kespry, Parrot, Yuneec, Autel Robotics, Pix4D, Insitu are some other prominent drone companies.

For many years, data giants such as Google, Amazon and Uber have promised us delivery drones bringing goods to our doorsteps in a matter of minutes. Amazon might be the company most well-known for its public testing of drones with Amazon Air. However, the list of businesses using drones for a variety of reasons is growing. One such case that has received a lot of attention for online deliveries, is the Amazon Prime Air initiative to get packages to customers in 30 minutes or less using drones.

Until recently, drones have tended to be either highly regulated or barely regulated at all. By and large, it has been a story of extremes: either drones have been deployed in specific circumstances by the military or flown during the weekend by hobbyists in their back gardens. That is set to change in the coming years thanks to a combination of legislation, a growing desire to deploy drones in the commercial sector and new international standards.

A number of early-adopter organizations are piloting or rolling out drones, particularly within sectors as diverse as real estate, construction, infrastructure, emergency services, filming and photography. Drones are already being used by the military and combatants in war zones and border-patrol forces for mapping and collecting security data.

The main economic benefits associated with drones are typically cost reduction and dispute resolution. Some of the most common applications of drones are geographical mapping, agricultural survey, disaster management, search and rescue, flood management, border patrol, anti-terror operations, maritime surveillance, critical infrastructure monitoring, intel gathering and others.

## Drones: Less-Than-Perfect Systems

Let us think why drones are taking so long to arrive as the new normal. There is a one-word answer: regulation. If our skies are to become as crowded as our streets and roads, airspace rules need updating to prevent accidents, terrorist attacks and other such related problems. The most important impact of all might be noise pollution.

Further, many unforeseen situations that arise during deliveries are managed by people. As drones are replacing the delivery people, they will need to be equipped to respond to such unforeseen incidents. From calculating where to drop the packages to preventing systems being hijacked by hackers, these are some of the major concerns with automated deliveries that need to be resolved before they can be widely adopted.

By the time your grandchildren grow up, there will be an entirely different scenario. As the drone-delivery system becomes ubiquitous, there will be huge competition. Not only will brands compete to get your attention, but delivery-service platforms will also join the rush. All this technological sophistication will certainly improve the quality of our life. But most of us will never realize the real price of this type of technology—humans.

# 11

# Internet in Our Bodies?

As we saw in the last two chapters, both transportation and delivery systems will be automated in the future through drones and driverless vehicles. This is possible because AI is present not only on the Internet and accessible through computers, but it is fast becoming a part of devices all around us. Thanks to this technology, our television, healthcare, clothing, aircrafts, refrigerators, cars and homes can connect to the Internet and be managed remotely.

Remote controlling takes over the operation of things from ovens and air conditioners to talking refrigerators. People's access to your home can also be remotely monitored through the Internet, so that even a stranger can temporarily be given entry into your home. Smart clothing makes the clothes on your back as smart as the phone in your pocket—your socks, shoes, sleepwear, can also go electronic. The clothing, which is machine washable, has copper wire built into it and a wireless charging pad is stitched inside a pocket. You can charge iPhones and Android phones through the built-in wireless charging capability.

As you have smart shopping, devices and appliances at your home know what you want even before you know it. Smart cars always keep you connected on the road—you can start the engine and set the temperature from a remote location. You can operate autonomous cars, locate traffic congestion, spot a parking space from remote locations and create a quality urban life. Smart aircraft invade your sky with drones, and gift boxes, household appliances and apparel are delivered by air. Smart warfare uses machines against your enemies, and you can manage the combatants from a remote location. Smart medicine brings you AI doctors that measure breathing, heart rate and muscle tension to determine a number of health and wellness metrics like stress level, activity, anxiety and predict what you should do even before you develop any health problems. Smart businesses give you opportunities to do business even without your physical presence by machines that can operate without humans. Smart cities come into reality where everyone is digitally connected.

As computers become smaller and cheaper, we will start seeing them in more places. A washing machine is already a computer that cleans clothes. In the future, you might not be able to buy a sensor-free T-shirt, and by then, you will take it for granted that your washing machine communicates with the clothes it is washing and automatically determines the optimal cycle and detergent to use. Then, the washing machine manufacturer will sell the information about what you are wearing and no longer wearing to clothing manufacturers.

We are reaching a fundamental shift where everything is becoming one complex, connected network system. There is more to this trend than the IoT. Humans are just another component in many of these systems. We provide inputs to these computers and accept their outputs. We are the consumers of their automated functionality. We affect these systems and we are thereby affected by them.

This thrilling piece of technology is maturing at an unparalleled rate, connecting innumerable objects in an all-encompassing network. The Internet is now stepping out from the realm of traditional PC and getting into every possible device owned by a human.

## What Is the Internet of Things?

IoT is basically the practice of connecting, monitoring and managing your 'things' or devices remotely. It is the ability to integrate your physical devices with your digital systems, to analyse those devices and the data between them to garner insights into what is happening in your environment, and to process those events and take actions as necessary. Kevin Ashton, a British technology pioneer who co-founded the Auto-ID Center at the Massachusetts Institutes of Technology (MIT), first used the term 'Internet of Things' in 1999.[79]

To give you an example, you probably have a phone that is constantly connected to the Internet. Then, there is a multitude of smart devices being pushed into the consumer market. These devices connect to your phone and your phone to the Internet. That is a small example of IoT—things talking to each other and over the Internet with other things.

IoT is dubbed the future of technology. The concept behind IoT is about connecting almost everything to the Internet. Typical examples are cars, industrial sensors, street lights, parking space, microwave ovens, door locks, power plants, heating systems, bathroom scales, and more. But many unexpected products are now getting Internet-connected too, like bridges, waste bins and even the soil in farmers' fields. Even wild tigers in Bandipur, elephants in Muthanga and Asiatic lions in Gir will become Internet-connected. The animals will be equipped with Internet-connected GPS trackers, enabling forest officials to monitor them from their smartphones in an attempt to support wildlife conservation and prevent poaching.

In a nutshell, everything will be linked, and each individual item will be able to recognize the other. An intelligent agent emerges when several inputs intermingle, which is the idea behind

IoTs where several objects are connected to a unified processing centre.

We believe that with IoT, the future will be beautiful, and we can't wait for it to get here. Big companies are beginning to recognize this advancement in technology and see the value it can add to them. They are now beginning to invest significantly into IoT, so that they can sell even more of their software to customers and harvest much more data in the process.

## Why IoT?

The management consulting firm McKinsey made a prediction for one trillion Internet-connected devices by 2025.[80] The global IoT market size was $308.97 billion in 2020. *Fortune Business Insights,* in a report, predicted that the market will become $1,854.76 billion in 2028 at a compound annual growth rate (CAGR) of 25.4 per cent in the 2021–28 period.[81] The global IoT market is expected to reach a value of $1,386.06 billion by 2026, according to Mordor Intelligence.[82] Reports indicated the number of IoT-connected devices such as cars, washing machines and refrigerators was 35.82 billion in 2021, and it will grow all the way to 75.44 billion by 2025.[83]

The number of things connected to the Internet is more than the number of people connected to it. This number will keep on increasing in the years to come. Many apps in smartphones have sequential impacts on our routine life. Many devices will become more familiar of us than members in the family. Job hunt, traffic, transport and logistics, insurance, healthcare, education, food safety, document management, security—are all a slurry of things in the physical world having life-changing impacts with the rapid use of the Internet for our everyday life. A totalizing effect on life is being seen with the growing Internet use.

Unless you come from an IT or cloud computing background,

you might not have heard of big data and predictive analytics. But trust me, you will hear these buzzwords a lot more in the future. Even now, all of the data you generate from your smartphone, computer and other devices is being used for purposes you may not be aware of. As the number of devices connected to the Internet grows, so, too, will the data they collect.

## Where Can IoT Be Applied?

The applications of IoT are found in almost all domains of life, including business, manufacturing, healthcare, retail, security and transport. The applications of IoT in key areas have been explained in the following description.

With IoT, you can switch on the air conditioning before reaching home or switch off the lights even after you have left home. Smart home appliances save time, energy and money. Washers and dryers can work with smart meters to obtain data on energy-use patterns and, after a particular period of time, operate without human intervention. Floor vacuuming and food-chopping can be performed by smart appliances. These smart appliances are empowered with an Internet connection, sensors and algorithms, and they can gather data about daily usage patterns and store the data online so that it is easily accessible and retrieve it for future operations. So, they can use the information gathered to schedule their own work intelligently.

Wearables from companies such as Fitbit, Google and Samsung have grown very popular. Wearable devices are installed with sensors and software that collect health and fitness data about the users. This data is processed to extract essential insights about the user. Wearable devices are highly energy-efficient and small-sized.

Smartwatches, sunglasses and clothes are convenient and hands-free alternatives to your common smartphone or tablet.

For example, in the event of an emergency, a smartwatch wearer can contact pre-set friends or family members in sequential order with the press of a button. This makes communication through the watch just like speaking through a phone. At the moment, there are smartwatches that allow parents to know the location and movement of their family members through GPS tracking. Smart glasses are another example of hands-free smartphone-like wearables.

Smart surveillance, automated transportation, smarter energy management systems, water distribution, urban security and environmental monitoring are examples of IoT applications for smart cities. IoT will solve major problems faced by the people living in cities with issues of pollution, traffic congestion and shortage of energy supply. Products like communication-enabled BigBelly trash cans will send alerts to municipal services when a bin needs to be emptied. By installing sensors and using web applications, citizens can find available parking slots across the city. Also, the sensors can detect meter-tampering issues, general malfunctions and any installation issues in the electricity system.

Smart farming is one of the fastest-growing fields in IoT. Farmers are using meaningful insights from the data to yield better returns on investment. Sensing for soil moisture and nutrients, controlling water usage for plant growth and determining custom fertilizers are some simple usages of IoT.

IoT provides an opportunity to retailers to get connected with the customers to enhance the in-store experience. Smartphones will be the way for retailers to remain connected with their consumers, even out of the store. They can also track the consumer's path through a store and improve store layout and place premium products in high-traffic areas.

The concept of a smart grid is becoming very popular all over the world. The basic idea behind smart grids is to automatically collect data and analyse the behaviour of electricity consumers and suppliers for improving efficiency as well as the economics of electricity usage. Smart grids will also be able to detect sources of power outages more quickly and at individual household levels like a nearby solar panel, making possible a distributed energy system. A smart thermostat can use sensors and predictive algorithms to detect when no one is at home and adjust the temperature accordingly to preserve energy.

Healthcare remains the sleeping giant of IoT applications. IoT in healthcare is aimed at empowering people to live healthier lives by wearing Internet-connected devices. The collected data will help in personalized analysis of an individual's health and provide tailor-made strategies to combat illness. Devices are connected to hospitals, doctors and relatives to alert them of medical emergencies and take preventive or necessary measures.

Livestock monitoring is about animal husbandry and cost-saving. Using IoT applications to gather data about the health and well-being of the cattle, ranchers know early about the sick animal which can be pulled out and help prevent large numbers of sick cattle. With the help of data, ranchers can also increase poultry production.

Smart dust consists of sensors at the nanotechnology level that can be deployed in the millions to billions, with a myriad of applications. They are computers smaller than a grain of sand and can be sprayed or injected almost anywhere to measure chemicals in the soil or to diagnose problems in the human body. These devices are the wave of the future for everything from global weather management and smart-city monitoring to war theatre mapping and internal medicine. They are a single package with sensing, computation, communication and power to collect data and report it back to the control centre.

Other applications of IoT include detection of river floods, landslides and earthquakes in advance, monitoring of snow level, measuring and control of air and water pollution, forest fire detection, leakage detection in water-transmission systems, identification of radiation levels, explosives and hazardous gases, and smart rescue systems.

In a nutshell, IoT is about the value, insights and opportunities gained from the interconnectivity of your physical and digital worlds. Depending on your specific needs, value can come in various forms. For example, if your needs include the tracking and monitoring of fleets of vehicles, your value could come in the form of driver compliance, route optimization, improved fuel efficiency and more accurate scheduling. If your needs include autonomously monitoring the health of a loved one or a patient, your value could come in the form of keeping them healthy and even alive.

## The Human Consequences

At present, mobile phones have become extensions of our physical appearance. But in future, devices that can be connected to the Internet will increase. Our clothes, wristwatch, ornaments, footwear, car, toothbrush and plenty of other things will become computational devices with access to the Internet.

Your whole life will become a computer on the Internet. Your oven is a computer that makes things hot. Your refrigerator is a computer that keeps things cold. Your camera is a computer with a lens and a shutter. An ATM is a computer with money inside. Modern light bulbs are computers that shine brightly. Your car is a computer system with four wheels and an engine. Your phone and television set at home are powerful computers.

Soon, smart devices may even be embedded in our bodies. Modern pacemakers and insulin pumps are smart. Pills are becoming smart. Smart contact lenses will monitor your glucose levels and diagnose your glaucoma. Fitness trackers are capable of sensing the state of our body.

Objects are also getting smart. You can buy a smart collar for your dog and a smart toy for your cat. You can buy a smart pen, a smart toothbrush, a smart coffee cup, a smart sex toy, a smart Barbie doll, a smart tape measure and a smart sensor for your plants. You can even buy a smart motorcycle helmet that will automatically call an ambulance and text your family if you have an accident.

Your houses, cars and pockets will be filled with more and more Internet-connected things. All of this will be done with good intentions. Good intentions from the manufacturer and good intentions from you. People will buy those products either willingly or not completely knowing what these things do.

These products already have vulnerabilities and are more akin to be hacked by data thieves, even terrorists. Someone will find those bugs and holes in the programming. For example, people with wicked intentions might gain access to a car's braking or engine systems or to your gas oven and lighting system. They might gain control of a house boiler and heating system. The casualty is high. Risk is high. Vulnerabilities are high—and someone might die as a consequence.

At that point, we will come back to the questions: 'Is it really a good idea to have control of the refrigerator from my smartphone?' 'Is it necessary to remotely turn on the AC?' 'Do we really need to unlock the door from a remote location?' It is now a good time to examine where this technology is going and ask some serious questions as to how the IoT may benefit, but also adversely affect society.

The Internet is disrupting the established rules that control the way we live our lives. From business to entertainment to government, we have already experienced the far-reaching effects of a technology that connects us in unprecedented ways.

Now, with the advent of the IoT, 'connection' is evolving beyond our mobile phones, tablets and computers. Our relations, emotions and values, and the whole world has been reduced to just numbers.

In popular media, any new technology tends to be treated with much enthusiasm, as if all new innovation is a good thing and should be pursued without restraint or regulation. If you examine the recent history of the Internet, it is clear it has brought many benefits to us all, and has become an indispensable tool used by millions of people on a daily basis. The Internet has caused seismic shifts in the way we communicate, work, consume information, protect and entertain ourselves. It has also made digital media freely accessible, often at no cost.

On the other hand, we must not overlook the disruptive effect it has had on society and businesses all over the world. It can be argued that although we enjoy the fruits of the Internet, it has created a society where jobs are increasingly outsourced to low-cost countries with dubious human rights and environmental policies. Valuable content is easily pirated, thereby depriving the creators of a living and makes information harder to trust due to the sheer unfiltered volume of it. IoT reduces our life to just numerals, which, in turn, replaces the human element in life and we will become more and more robot-like. Our actions, behaviour, feelings and social relations will be controlled by algorithms which give us pre-set behaviour through calculations. And we respond the way they want us to behave. Do we really want that?

# 12

## Custom-Generated Thoughts

I know people who, by their choice, tend to be comfortable with people and things they like on the Internet. By choice, they never opt for people and information that stand opposite to their convictions. There are people I have known for many years who network on their social media profiles with people they think almost endorse the same ideas, share the same interest and have political leanings that conform to their own. I know people endorsing Left-leaning political views subscribe to news sources that strengthen their conviction. I know rightists and centrists doing the same. I know casteists following casteists, Dalits following Dalits, communalists following communalists, writers following writers and journalists following other journalists. The Internet has a peculiar feature in which you can follow things you like while distancing away from those you dislike. It is okay to choose what you like and it's your right, but the damage it does to your thinking mind cannot be underestimated.

As discussed earlier, the average person with Internet access in India lives in an information bubble. The Internet has reduced their life such that their personal beliefs and convictions are perpetuated no matter what. They tend to mingle with people having similar interests, tastes and the like. People with dissenting convictions are not entertained. The small screen that you are holding on your palm is a window to the echo chambers where people become obsessed with themselves. They connect with people they like and look for opinions they already agree with. On Facebook and Twitter, you follow the content that you like, while distancing yourself from what you dislike. On YouTube, you watch content that you like. For news, you subscribe to online news channels that you think caters to your liking.

That said, when the Internet started in India in 1995, that was not the situation. Optimism about its power was huge. People believed it would disseminate unheard voices to a huge audience and reach out far to the unreached. It was okay to think along those lines. There was no Trump. No Brexit. No Cambridge Analytica. Elon Musk and Stephen Hawking didn't make comments about doomsday scenarios following AI. Facebook hadn't started selling user data to third parties. Fake news didn't get invented nor had post-truth become an obsession in the western world. Whistle-blower Christopher Wylie hadn't compared the Facebook data scandal with modern-day colonialism. While writing this book in 2019, all these events had happened. Eli Pariser has written about the bubble effect of the Internet. Increasingly, we are finding ourselves pushed into such Internet bubbles—little groups of like-minded people or 'echo chambers'.

For example, the micro-blogging site Twitter allows its users to build an active network by connecting with other Twitter users. You can follow posts by others and subscribe to them. Twitter was one of the first social media sites to offer the concept of hashtags. Despite the heavy use of hashtags, it can lead to a filter bubble effect. It's a situation in which content embedded with these hashtags mound on our news feed. The accumulation of content that we like is associated with a problem called confirmation bias. We will have a tendency to favour and reuse only those items that confirm what we already believe. This scenario works not only in business and commerce but even in political processes. The whole idea of the hashtag is to enable you to find tweets and updates on Facebook timelines and other information sources that interest you. It is a simple and fast-sorting mechanism. This phenomenon is called filter bubble. Filter bubbles are seen as critical enablers of Brexit, Trump, Bolsonaro and other popular political phenomena all over the world. Twitter users interested in political tweets of Donald Trump, the former US president, would be stuck either with pro-Donald Trump hashtags such as #MAGA or anti-Trump hashtags, say #fakepresident. This is an example of a filter bubble associated with hashtags on Twitter.[84] At the same time, you can also avoid those that bother you. The concern towards the filter bubble invading our cognitive skills received wider public attention with the publication of *The Filter Bubble* by Eli Pariser, *The Net Delusion* by Evgeny Morozov, *The Shallows* by Nicholas Carr and *So You've Been Publicly Shamed* by Jon Ronson.

## The Basics

Introduced and popularized by the US technology entrepreneur and activist Eli Pariser, mostly through his 2011 book *The Filter Bubble*[85] and other popular essays, the coinage 'filter bubble' speculates an algorithmic scenario all of us are experiencing. The information search results displayed by search engines like Google are a 'personalized universe of information'. We have no control over what we see. Is there any problem with it? Of course. The information world in which we are living differ from individual to individual. It is an imposing concept that suggests that search engines and social media recommendations are accountable for the ideological and social polarization in many societies. We are not exposed to balanced and healthy information. We see information that reinforces our established worldviews. Information is tailor-made for each universe.

It was generally understood that Pariser failed to provide a clear definition for this term and it remained vague, founded only on anecdotes without being empirically substantiated. The concept didn't prevent it from gaining huge interest and widespread currency in empirical and scientific discourses. Now, journalists, writers, politicians, influencers, activists and advocates are accused of living in a filter bubble. It is argued that they are seeing only what they like and it prevents them seeing the concerns of others. Their empathetic mind is spoiled by the filter bubble.

Today, we can see the filter bubble as more akin to disruptions in flow in our information universe of social media. This change in focus is an indication of the increasing role of social media as an important news source. The filter-bubble concept is increasingly aligned with a similar concept of echo chambers. Scholarly and popular articles now use the two concepts interchangeably to refer to almost the same scenario.[86] A clear distinction between the two concepts was made difficult by both Pariser and the famous legal scholar Cass Sunstein, who never defined the term with empirical evidence in his book *Echo Chambers*.[87]

The Internet has a peculiar facility of narrowing fields of vision, diluting diversities and potentially creating echo chambers of reinforced belief. It means that if you habitually come across certain websites, friends or online content with likes or emojis, frequently share that content on your Facebook page and Twitter, then these data giants know what type of things you are highly engaged with. So, it gives you more of the stuff with which you would engage more and less of the stuff with which you would least engage.

Data giants design their algorithms to provide the tools to let you avoid anything that you don't like. Thus, it confines you to online bubbles of personally tailored information content that make you feel safe and give you peace of mind. This feature allows them to keep you engaged on their sites for longer. That is just what they want too. So long as you remain on their platform, the market value of such sort of service providers increases.

Now, all of us have the tools to publish whatever we want to. There are no editors filtering content on its veracity. It is easy to find content to substantiate almost any way of thinking, no matter how negative or biased. All of us end up finding the narrative that is most consistent with our system of beliefs.

The filter bubble potentially pushes moderates into more extreme ways of thinking and polarizing our society. It thickens your casteist mind. It increases your sexist attitudes. It also helps spread misinformation and fake news. If you spend all day receiving content from trusted friends, you are less likely to develop the healthy skepticism that is necessary to consider the veracity of a story before you share it.

After all is said, there is a dangerous element being hidden. All the things you subscribe and follow is your personal choice. But what if content carriers try to give us only those which, according to their learnt understanding, is what we tend to like? The result is cognitive disaster.

## The Impacts

There is a danger. Those who upload digital content can do much more than those who read or see it. The unknown forces that control and manipulate the universe of information lie in a space where somebody creates content to be received by others at a delivery point. It means we get information we never intend to get through. You can view it as a filter bubble in its most alarming proportion.

In the days ahead, each of us will live in our own distinct information universe—caste bubbles, class bubbles, gender bubbles, profession bubbles, language bubbles and plenty of others. We will receive information that is pleasing, familiar and entertaining. We will never know what is being hidden from us. There will be less room for the unexpected adventures and emergencies that are scenarios which spark creativity and exchange of ideas in humans.

This kind of information filtering has done considerable damage not only generally to our democracy but to the plight of Dalits, women and minorities. Now, information seekers customize information based on what is interesting and uninteresting. They follow Narendra Modi but unfollow Rahul Gandhi. Those following the Congress do not follow the BJP. Those following secularists do not follow communalists. Therefore, the filter bubble has polarized and divided information sharing, which is the central element of democracy. We become so secure in our bubbles that we start accepting only that information, no matter if it is true or not, which confirms our assumptions. We can call it confirmation bias, which is a phrase coined by English psychologist Peter Wason.[88] People tend to favour information that confirms or strengthens their pre-existing beliefs or ideas. Such ideas and values, once affirmed, are most unlikely and difficult to remove.

# 13

# Information Cartels

For the majority of us, the Internet is what we take more than what we give. That is, we are more aware and concerned with the information we take from the Internet than what we give to it. However, what we give is more important for service providers, even though we care little for it. But there is a danger in this attitude. For example, one may Google the keywords: 'Leading politicians in India'. The search engine, which is an intelligent machine, brings in millions of results within less than a second. The query leads us to the platforms of the big players in the top of the search results: *Business Standard*, *The Times of India*, *The Indian Express*, just to cite a few examples, which carry information about your query. Try searching on Google with the key words: 'Leading female politicians in India', you will get the results of pages from *India Today*, *DNA* and *Deccan Herald*.

Just a couple of outlets on the Internet receive the majority of search traffic and audience, while the mass of individual publishers, self-broadcasters, private narratives and personal stories do not attract followers. The Internet has metamorphosed into a playground for few big players: Google, Amazon, Apple, Facebook, Twitter, YouTube, and a couple of other big names. Very few people have become successful on the Internet, where big tech companies dominate. Be it health and wellness, sports, arts and entertainment, fashion, automobile and tech reviews, or foodie space, influencers who enjoy commanding heights within their niche in conventional ways are still someone their audiences seek for information, insights and directions, with rare exceptions. These influencers still hold their visibility among their audience in the Internet space.

## Digital Apartheid?

When I searched for the keyword 'corruption', I found a blogger who had posted articles of excellent quality. You would get a lot of well-written essays on his blog called Thoughts. In October 2012, he had posted a note on corruption titled 'Is Corruption an Issue in Indian Politics?'[89] By December 2014, over a period of two years, the blog had received just six comments. I shared the post on my personal Facebook page; till October 2018, the link has received not a single 'like'.

But for the same keyword search, 'corruption', I got a webpage (www.nitinpai.in) which posted a commentary on corruption titled 'Why Anna Hazare is wrong and Lok Pal a bad idea'.[90] It was posted on 14 August 2011. By December 2014, it had received a huge number of likes and shares on the Internet. I searched some other web pages and Facebook communities with the same keyword as well. Within no time after the publication, the post in *The Times of India*'s online edition, 'Anna Hazare's movement is anti-social justice, manuwadi'[91] had received huge online traffic by December 2014. The Facebook page 'India Against Corruption' received 1.5 million likes and the Facebook page 'Anna Hazare' had 7 lakh likes by 2014.

In January 2014, when I Googled with the keywords 'Democracy in India', the result I got was over 130 million pages in less than a second. However, pages piloted by bigger outlets such as *The Times of India* and *The Hindu* were listed at the top. This means that search engines cruise users to a certain pattern of web pages. Such outlets, in fact, understand how to manipulate search traffic and increase the number of visitors to their sites.

The above-mentioned blog Thoughts and Biju Gayu (bijugayu.blogspot.com), my personal blog, are two similar stories—the exclusion and digital apartheid that takes place on the Internet. Some platforms have a large readership while others do not, regardless of the quality of the content.

### Testing the Online Readership

The websites Merinews (merinews.com) and India Opines (indiaopines.com) are citizen journalism platforms, which may have shut down by the time this book is published. I ran experiments on these platforms from December 2012 to January 2014 as part of the investigation on the concept of information cartels. In December 2012, I posted an article on Merinews titled 'Internet activism is a myth'.[92] By December 2014, it had grabbed close to 500 shares. Though miniscule compared to other bigger platforms, I was happy that at least someone had read the article. If I had posted it on my personal academic blog, I am convinced that I would not have gotten as many readers.

I published more than 30 articles on Merinews (www.merinews.com/cj/bijupr) and four articles on the opinion blog, India Opines (indiaopines.com/author/bijup/). The purpose of the continuous submission of opinion articles over this period was to dispel a popular perception—the internet is an alternative space. We think that all social groups, irrespective of their socially disadvantageous positions, are able to find their voices heard on the Internet. But it's a myth. The Internet is not a space that provides avenues and platforms to previously marginalized groups of people.

In a short time, the trend was clear. Despite all the efforts on content contribution on these platforms, I was publishing on online domains, which indeed do not have a sizeable readership. The fact was that, although I published over 80,000 words on Merinews, among which the majority of the contributions were critiques of the Internet, political class and democracy, I got roughly 3,000 shares for all the posts, which includes Facebook likes, Tweets, etc., on the Internet platforms aforesaid. Sadly, the Internet traffic received on these platforms was discouraging.

I published four opinion articles on India Opines, and this outlet, in fact, had over 420,000 likes on its Facebook page in January 2018. Interestingly, I got quite a few readers and roughly 20 shares for each post on India Opines.

If no one reads my blog, the first thing I need to ask myself is, 'Am I alone in the connected space?' No one listens to you on the Internet, nor do you have huge followers on social media profiles. Most people on the Internet have no audience nor likes, shares or comments. Your updates, opinions and other kinds of postings attract not more people than hands have fingers.

## Information Cartels: Do They Exist?

Algorithms and data analytics, through default-set search engines, take user searches to a couple of information cartels. Ad strategies are so designed that every user-search lands where the market wants us to. What we search is not necessarily what we actually need. We are made to think in a particular way by AI and at a more basic level, machine learning. There is an unholy nexus between technology companies and monopolies. Here, connection technologies said to be alternative spaces seldom exist. They have developed human-like intelligence, at least in part. Hence, they have conquered our cognitive power.

Look at the winner-takes-all websites. A bird's eye view, for example, of an article posted on big outlets, such as

*The Times of India*, *Hindustan Times*, *The Hindu* would surely get a whopping number of likes, shares and comments within a few hours, which the lone individual broadcasters and online writers would not get on the Internet.

The fact is clear: quality, originality and source are not necessarily the mark of online visibility. Traffic for online content is clearly a conspiracy. You keep getting newer apps for different activities on the Internet, but this does not necessarily mean that you are doing some amazing things; it implies that you should participate in it with Google, Facebook and Twitter. It is to make you believe that there is no choice, but only a 'bigger choice'. Facebook, Google, Twitter, YouTube, WhatsApp and a couple of other players are your bigger choice.

Life on the Internet is fast moving to information cartels.[93] Search engines, which are configured by machine learning technology, drive users to outlets which they do not intend to visit. This sort of information cartels are deliberate and a manipulation of user behaviour by way of paid campaigning and ad wars.

## The Internet Is Not a Democratic Tool

Contrary to lingering popular beliefs, the Internet has done little to condense democratic engagements and mature political dialogue, but, in fact, has instead empowered a posse of elites. They are arguably the so-called celebrity class on Twitter, the successful timeline warriors of the crowd class on Facebook, trendsetting top-notch YouTubers, the so-called professional elites on LinkedIn, and so on.

Celebrities and youth icons are colonizing the Internet space with a huge fan following. Sports stars are a boisterous Facebook choice on social media profiles. YouTube materials of film stars and female sports stars get innumerably large fan clicks. Their

YouTube clips get comments, most of which must be censored.

The verified Facebook page of Deepika Padukone, the Bollywood star, has 49 million followers and her Twitter profile has 27.6 million followers as of January 2022. Indian cricketer Sachin Tendulkar has over 37 million followers on Facebook and 36.7 million followers on Twitter. Tendulkar's timeline activities get thousands of likes, comments and shares, for each update.

Olympic gold-medallist Neeraj Chopra was the most-searched personality in India in 2021 on Google. Virat Kohli and MS Dhoni dominated the search results for sports personalities. Yahoo's Year in Review 2021 lists Kareena Kapoor Khan as the most-searched female film celebrity.[94] Corruption, Aam Aadmi Party (AAP), education, unemployment and rape are among the few major keywords most people searched on the Internet in India. Rape, for example, gets one over 796 million results (in 0.48 seconds).

The Internet is reinforcing privileged voices in society, while suppressing any attempt at opening the process to more diverse voices. We live in the bailiwick of information colonizers, ruled by search engines and digital media technologies that mull over attention to just a handful of 'push-button strategists', 'track-pad swipers' and 'winner-takes-all' websites. The idea that alternative media is empowering more and more ordinary people to become go-ahead political participants in the process is mostly a fable.

The Web 2.0[95] presence of big players, such as publishing outfits, news bureaus, monopolists, marketers and big-name corporates corroborates the fact that big players that have been monopolizing the democratic space before the onset of the Internet are going to maintain their colonies on a connected space as well.

The higher concentration of big outlets in terms of search traffic and perspective generation has created a highly manipulative agenda-setting mechanism. That is, what to discuss, how to think, where to communicate, etc. are negotiated by just a few websites, concentrated only among key groups. Policy decisions are most influenced by those key players. They have a higher number of followers, likes and shares on Twitter, Facebook, LinkedIn and Instagram.

An elite few are the agenda setters on the Internet. They arguably comprise information and power elites. The top educated, inbuilt intelligentsia and elites are most popular on the Internet. Most frequently, the male, upper class, upper caste, less ethnically diverse and with less plural political commentaries decide the agenda on Internet platforms and become hit makers. A few opinion shapers manufacture the opinions of the majority of those on connected space.

Net neutrality was a hot new subject in India while I was in the finishing stages of this chapter. Net neutrality is the concept that Internet service providers such as BSNL, Jio and Vi require to treat all data on the Internet equally. Sometimes, service providers charge some companies for the huge traffic they cause on the network. Facebook Zero, Wikipedia Zero, and Google Free Zone are examples of net neutrality. Some big players are becoming fatter day by day on the Internet. Now, the new war is between one set of service providers (think of internet service provider—ISP) such as Airtel, Reliance, etc. and the other set of providers say Facebook, Twitter, Flipkart, Amazon, Google, etc. How would you feel if one set of providers asks for a profit share from the other set of service providers, for the reason that the successful margin of the latter was because of the former? The claim is that the former argues that the latter is successful because of them, as they provide Internet connectivity. It looks as if one was claiming a portion of their margin from the other. With this debate going on, Airtel has launched Airtel Zero. Facebook launched Internet.org, tying up with Reliance. Many players are eyeing to swallow the Internet.

The Internet is now colonized by cartels. There is no more free space.

# 14

# Our 'Datafied' Life

Imagine this scenario: your college is a hundred years old, and every year, 700 students are admitted. The data inventory of the college records the demographic of its newcomers. Demographic relates to the structure of a population, which deals with factors like age, name, race, language, marital status, children, parental details, sex, income and other personal details. The data entered is structured. So, if you want to know the details of a student admitted in a particular year, the data inventory will find you the same quickly. If you want to know the details of the caste population admitted over a particular decade, the inventory will fetch you the details. Income group, place, region, gender—you can draw many patterns for a period of time from this inventory. From all the demographic profiles of people over the hundred years, the information you source from the inventory helps you draw some propositions.

Imagine another scenario. You are doing a survey of gender discrimination in Indian households. You have a sample frame in which two states, each from the northern, southern, western and eastern parts of India is selected. As you enter the demographics into a computer software for processing, it is easy to find patterns based on region, class, education, marital status, employment and others. You can propose concepts according to the data stored.

It is also easy for traditional computer software to process and find patterns out of the demographics entered. But, your data inventory does not give you psychographics of the population, which deals with attitudes, interests, personality, values, opinions and lifestyle. It is also difficult for an ordinary software-enabled data inventory to give you qualitative elements of a population from its data feed.

## Data Firms Have Inventories of All of Us

Think about a similar scenario in the age when data firms control us. Facebook, Twitter, YouTube, Google, Instagram, WhatsApp, Amazon, Uber and others have millions of users. All of us engage in the sort of activities for which each of them was created. We like, post, comment, share, reply and discuss.

On Facebook, you post opinions, upload photos, share links, give likes, network with people, talk to friends, give comments to other people's activities, post reviews about a product and plenty of other things. On Twitter, you tweet, retweet and post your opinion and engage in other things you are interested in. You follow your favourite actors, writers and leaders. You engage with different things on Twitter. On YouTube, you watch your favourite videos, watch brand reviews, listen to music, watch movies, watch your favourite dancers, listen to speakers, and many other kinds of activities. On Instagram, you post pictures of almost everything you have captured on frame. On Amazon, you give reviews to the footwear you recently purchased.

You recently travelled to Kolkata, where you had plenty of rides with Uber and did the same with Ola on another recent journey to Patna. Recently, you booked food on Swiggy and bought a churidar for your wife on Myntra. Enormous user data is being generated from all these activities.

Every day, we are increasingly depending on such technologies for activities we thought no technology is required at all. Now, we are heavily dependent on them. The companies that give us services on their platforms at the same time track our behaviour as we make our way across their services. They try to understand what we really want, what we really do and who we really are. It is easily doable for them as we constantly make us of their platforms.

Our activities are digitized, which creates a huge inventory of information in the form of data. When we fill a government form giving our name, age, caste and income details, we are aware that you are sharing information about yourself. In the digital era, digital platforms and virtual spaces become an extension of our everyday physical space. What makes it different from physical space is the mediation. That it takes place on a platform owned, operated and collaborated with various other parties, which provides us with their privacy policy along with terms and conditions before using any of the platforms that each one of us has to agree for using. Our interactions, networking, transactions, personal details, etc. get left behind on this space each time we log out. We may be out of it, but we still live in it. The next time you log in, the notification of where you left the last time shows up, or say for instance in the case of a news app, algorithms feed you with the type of news that you viewed last day. It reminds you of who you are even if you want to start afresh the new day. The data we generate is so large that it cannot be processed through simple data management systems. It is too big to be processed using traditional database and software techniques. It consists of billions to trillions records of millions of people. One striking feature of all this data being generated is that it is created not by digital companies, but by users. The data is so loosely structured that it is often incomplete and incomprehensible.

## We Are 'Datafied'

What makes big data unique? As in the case of the college survey, the data does not get enough access to the inner mind of a population by collecting demographics. But, in contrast, data firms get access to the cognitive mind as they deploy psychographics. What makes big data unique then is the fact that it is huge, accessible, quick, cheap and credible. Most importantly, it's a gateway to our thinking mind.

In many ways, big data has improved our lives. But whether we as individuals benefit from this wealth of data to the maximum possible is a tough question. For example, be it a bank evaluating our credit worth, an insurance company determining our risk level or an employer deciding whether we get a job, the data we generated is likely used against us rather than for us.

Big data certainly helps in reducing transaction costs and enhancing cross-border flow of money. Data has grown in nearly every part of our lives from gene sequencing to consumer behaviour. Large chunks of our social, economic and political life have moved digital.

We are 'datafied'. Our everyday life is 'datafied'. Datafication is, however, not only about people starting to do things online but also about people doing new things.

Just like electrical appliances did help us, the tools made available to us, thanks to big data, deeply influence our life. But however grateful we are to dishwashers and washing machines for helping us with our daily drudgery, do we need them as our life partners? Not at all. Let us then ask, no matter how grateful we are to the corporates using big data, such as Amazon and Google, are we really able to exercise the same choice for intelligent technologies with which we preferred how to live with other helpful tools like dishwashers? The answer is more likely to be negative.

Our new tools are becoming more human-like. Enabling this type of transformation are those tools which have a 'voice' and 'recognition' capabilities. They can speak and have voice-recognition capabilities. Your bots understand you, identify you and answer your needs. You don't even have to push buttons or type commands. You just call out the name, and the tool is at your service.

The purely human experience of conversation is now possible between humans and intelligent machines. The device sits modestly in your living room, kitchen, air conditioner, car and refrigerator. When devices listen and speak, a new relationship begins to form. This way of change in our life is a result not from the tools, but from our tendency to humanize everything—from birth to death.

The machines grow in their knowledge of you by processing data about you. They are listening and learning to serve you better. Such tools are designed from networks in our homes and other places, in much the same way our human brain functions. They soon know what you like and dislike, how you live, think, work and play. This is addictively convenient for us. But we are increasingly giving a warm welcome to big-data dictatorships.

The fundamental question is what happens when our social life is transformed into so much data. Data is not a mirror of the social. It represents the abstraction of everything from thoughts, emotions and facts into sets of computable numerals. What have we compromised through such a metamorphosis? What have we lost when the richness and complexity of the social that gets abstracted into data is ourselves? Our human skills are compromised. We don't know who grabs what kind of data from us and from where, when and how.

From state surveillance to the commodification of all aspects of social life, it appears that it is not simply data that is compromised. I feel that at the centre of our future remains a new relation: data relations. Big data arises from this expanded ability to collect, store, sort and analyse hints about our inner mind. Our mind is mined for drawing patterns about our behaviour that can be used for prediction. Video cameras watch our movements and private consumer data brokers map our interests and sell that information to data clients. Phone numbers, emails and finances can all be studied for various purposes. Government agencies collect health, educational and criminal records. Data miners monitor Facebook, YouTube and Twitter feeds. This is the big data world of data brokers. Still, this world is largely in its infancy but offering vastly new possibilities. Behind the big data is technology: algorithms, network analysis, data mining, machine learning and a host of computer technologies being refined and improved every day.

Several ethical challenges are posed by big data, which is even considered as a destroyer of informed consent, according to A. Michael Froomkin.[96] The data we leave when we engage with several stakeholders becomes the source of revenue for other entities. These are used by third parties without our consent, and at times for purposes other than what we have given consent to. It provides opportunities for generating unexpected insights even from unforeseen information.

# 15

## America Everywhere

The Chinese created the search engine Baidu as a substitute for Google for the Chinese market; similarly, the microblog Weibo for Twitter, the Renren social networking site for Facebook, the Alibaba e-commerce platform for Amazon and the Youku video-sharing site for YouTube. It seemed a thrilling response to western monopoly over social media.

Back in India, it is the opposite. India is one of the largest users of Facebook (241 million),[97] WhatsApp (close to 500 million),[98] Instagram (201 million)[99] and Twitter (24 million).[100] Flipkart outpaced Amazon India and AJIO in 2021 with the most number of downloads.[101] India is in a ride-sharing race on Uber with the US.[102] We are increasingly the market for western, primarily American, tech giants in terms of intelligent technologies. These technologies have a totalizing effect upon our living universe, which is already heavily Americanized. Intelligent technologies based on AI and data analytics are at the centre of this new trend. As we have seen earlier, the way we think, act, work and communicate are heavily influenced by these information cartels.

Unlike the Chinese, we have already fallen prey to the big platforms that have swallowed our socio-cultural milieu. We are increasingly being confronted with value systems totally alien to us, which are brought up to our world by these types of connection technologies.

## What Is Digital Colonialism?

The West came to America by boat from Europe in the past. Almost every country in the world was colonized at one point. Though most gained independence by the mid-twentieth century, colonialism is in no way a distant memory for nations as they still experience it in a new way.

At a more basic level, the current use of AI is helping the rise of data colonialism, which takes place when the technological solutions of the western world are imported to solve the problems of those societies that do not have technology, often without their consent. Through intelligent technologies of the West, our life is ostensibly subject to their intervention. It is within this context that plenty of literature from the global south views the expansion of intelligent technologies from the West with scepticism.[103]

Digital colonialism is the deployment of an invisible form of imperial power over a vast number of people. This control is exerted without the explicit consent of those over whom it is deployed. It is manifested in technological architecture, rules, designs, languages, cultures and belief systems by vastly dominant tech giants supported by their respective parent governments. Just as kingdoms and empires have expanded phenomenally through the control of some key factors such as trade routes to oceans, railways, roads and bridges and raw materials, there are now technology empires. These control data and computational power to dominate the world.

For example, by the end of 2011, the US State Department had spent $70 million on secret communication technologies to facilitate Internet activists to communicate beyond the reach of oppressive political systems.[104] It should be read alongside the then secretary of state, Hillary Clinton's warning that a 'new information curtain is descending across much of the world'. She was pointing towards China's hackers targeting Google in 2010.[105] Meanwhile, China issued a callous reply to the US establishments that expressed its concern over the imposing of 'information imperialism'[106] on China.[107]

Hillary Clinton, in a major speech on Internet freedom in January 2010, said, 'In the last year, we've seen a spike in threats to the free flow of information. China, Tunisia and Uzbekistan have stepped up their censorship of the Internet.'[108] Referring to social and economic development, the Internet can serve as a 'great equalizer', added Clinton in her speech. The message is clear that Internet freedom is the avowed goal of the US. However, behind the veil of this cry for freedom of the Internet, much remained unsaid.

Studies corroborated the fact that deregulated Internet has direct correlation with digital literacy projects such as pro-revolutionary blogging in countries like Kyrgyzstan, where the campaign has translated into a culture of communication practice that helped a statewide revolution in 2005 called the Tulip Revolution.[109] The US state department and US-based philanthropic organizations had a huge role in it. The US information intervention and US-backed operations of digital literacy in Syria, Tunisia and Egypt have serious implications for data colonialism.

## Isn't Digital Colonialism a Good Thing?

People are asking why it is necessary to present it in negative terms if somebody is happy using platforms like Facebook. However, the foundations of freedom and democracy are at stake when centralized global tech firms have the power to process, monitor and mediate all user data. They analyse personal data and make collective behaviour predictable. The knowledge is privatized and protected by trade secret laws. The point is that this type of data colonialism is also determining the lives of millions who do not use intelligent technologies.

The offline population is the disputed territory of tech empires. Those who get them locked into their digital control hold the key to the future. The proliferation of Internet-connected mobile phones, in theory, is bringing the world together. People living continents apart are talking and sharing. Fuelled by the sweet nectar of social apps, people across political boundaries feel they are constantly connected. But in some cases, these connections turn into collisions or clashes between different value systems. The impacts of data colonialism are exactly on the clashes of value systems in which local value systems are overtaken by value systems promoted by intelligent connection technologies.

## Value Conflicts

As the US exports intelligent connection technologies, its values confront local cultures. Instagram, Snapchat, Twitter and others have all had conflicts with the laws and cultural norms of local populations outside the US. Political authorities in different parts of the non-western world have started imposing punitive actions on various sections of people for doing things that are deemed to be non-western.[110]

In societies and communities where Islamic law prevails, Instagram has landed up in controversy several times, because it is not acceptable for women to share their picture publicly. Iranian authorities, for example, arrested young women and models who had been posting photos on Instagram claiming that they were 'promoting Western promiscuity'.[111]

What happens to the face-swap feature on Snapchat in a society where laws on morphing are strict and cultures where using somebody's images without consent amounts to a punishable offence? Face swap is a feature of digitally swapping the faces of two subjects in an image, for humorous effect. Indians, who use this tool to rope in satire into their content, face punitive actions. People are potentially in trouble for a unique issue in which India's laws around manipulating people's photos are strict. Morphing a face or image is bringing Snapchat's face-swap feature under legal scrutiny.[112]

What happens when people use Twitter and Facebook for political satire, criticism of ruling elites and political dissent? These platforms have also landed people into unwanted controversy. People are arrested for criticizing the government, ministers and other ruling elites. For example, a bunch of Twitter accounts were simultaneously deactivated because they all made fun of Putin and the Russian government. They were later reinstated without explanation.[113]

The culture clashes emerging from value systems coming out of technologies made in America are in some ways larger problems than the legal issues. Each platform has its own particular homegrown culture and value system. Twitter has always been a place for political satire, dialogues and critical engagements. Snapchat is disorderly, childish and, to some extent, celebrity obsessed. Instagram is slightly egotistic—a place where you curate a beauty-filtered version of your life, hiding the real *you*.

When used and popularized in cultures distinct from the ones in which these platforms were created, the data giants hold control at the cultural, intellectual and political level.

## American Culture Goes Global

The tech industry and Internet can bridge vast distances and connect cultures. It will be creating a new system of legal norms more uniform and homogenous throughout the world. But, as of yet, that is not how it has been playing out. This had always been an American vision and dream. It is a dream of the techno-libertarianism that was trying to force itself on the world as a global dream from the depths of Silicon Valley. Empires force their own ideals and values over existing cultures. This is the sort of colonialism in which one value system dominates over the rest. But this new form of colonialism is quite different.

The problem isn't that these companies export American technology; it is that they export American culture too. The controversies in India and rest of the world aren't fundamentally tech-related at all. They aren't issues that could be resolved with a faster network connection, universal access points, or cheaper smartphones for everyone. It is caused by a fundamental disconnect between the cultures and value systems each of these platforms create and celebrate. The traditional cultures and value systems that already exist are pushed aside in the new market world created by these big American tech giants.

## The Dark Side of Data Colonialism

However, the impacts of drone technology and mobile apps feel insignificant when compared to the revelations that clandestine corporations like Cambridge Analytica are distorting elections in Kenya, India and the Philippines. The news that public relations companies like Bell Pottinger are profiting from fanning the flames of ethnic tensions in South Africa and elsewhere is far more shocking than the impacts of technology.[114]

For several years now, we have been following Facebook's aggressive expansion into developing countries. A Global Voices report called it a form of 'digital colonialism'.[115] Facebook has expanded its global footstep using a cut-down 'Free Basics' version. *Foreign Policy* magazine called it 'a dictator's dream come true'.[116]

We have also seen resistance to these tactics, notably in India. The programme was overturned by net neutrality activists.[117] Then, recently, Facebook confessed that all 2 billion Facebook-user accounts worldwide are likely to have been compromised.[118] It also included those of 560,000 citizens in India.[119] It was confirmed that companies, including Cambridge Analytica, have been using the data to psychologically profile Facebook users in Indonesia and Malaysia, so that it can micro-target them with tailored messages to shape their thinking and voting behaviour. Whistle-blower Christopher Wylie described this as 'modern-day colonialism'.[120]

We now know, for example, that Cambridge Analytica was paid millions for just 90 days' work in Kenya, prior to Uhuru Kenyatta's contested re-election.[121] They were also employed during the elections in both India and the Philippines.[122] Cambridge Analytica is not alone in this business; Kenya's opposition party also employed the consulting firm, Aristotle.[123]

New evidence has also emerged that coordinated social media campaigns were specifically designed to enflame racial tensions in Myanmar,[124] Ethiopia[125] and in South Africa.[126] We learnt that it is not just Russia[127] and China[128] that train and employ troll farms and bot armies. It is increasingly hard to find any country in which State or non-State actors are not using trolls and bots to attack opposition candidates, spread fake news to cover open debates or inflict online gender-based violence on women activists and politicians. Many countries were using trolls and bots to shape people's thinking and frame online debates at home and abroad.

Colonizing minds is the end result of data colonialism. Shaping consciousness and controlling public debate is being insourced to secret services or military units and outsourced to firms like Cambridge Analytica. Troll farms and bot armies are available for hire and deployed anywhere, at anytime and on any issue. Digital colonialists do not need to go to the expense of physical colonization as they can further their interests and extend their power by colonizing minds rather than territories.

## The New Cultural Imperialism

In the twentieth century, the main culprit of undesirable values from outside was what sometimes is called 'cultural imperialism'. Pop culture products like rock 'n' roll, Pepsi, McDonalds and Hollywood films were seen as promoting dangerous individualism, a hatred of authority, and a love for consumerism and wealth.

Today, non-western countries are fighting the new battle: a culture clash in which the value system represented by connection technologies conflict with those of the native population. These values are arriving not through artworks and products made by others, but through a tool that locals can use themselves.

As of 2018, the leading tech giants, such as Google, Facebook, Yahoo, Apple, Microsoft, Uber, Amazon and Tesla, are the world's top tech companies by audience. Curiously enough, they were based in the US, but the majority of their users were not American.[129] This fact was made painfully obvious to those users and their governments when Edward Snowden's trove of the National Security Agency (NSA) documents showed just how American tech giants had stooped to cooperate with surveillance demands.

## Data Colonialism Promotes Homogeneity

A new generation of tech companies has overtaken industries like hospitality (Airbnb), transportation (Uber and Lyft), office space (WeWork) and more, bringing a set of tech-inflected values with them. Now, a tendency is ongoing in the way the public sphere is shaped across the world. In the process, social classes across the world are becoming ever more alike. The same profession, ideas, value systems and social practices, the world is shrinking because intelligent machines have conquered diversity, and in turn minimized it. The political structure is becoming increasingly similar. Political systems reflect similarity in the form of communication they incorporate, especially on social media. The trend towards global homogenization of media systems, the public sphere and political communication, apparently, has morphed into reinforcing an American ecosystem for political engagement.

The rising significance of digital computation and telecommunication is strongly associated with the coming in of a global culture mediated by intelligent technologies. This culture is at present under control by enterprises in the northern hemisphere and, in particular, the English-speaking nations—for instance, CNN, MTV, Disney, Intel, Murdoch, Microsoft, etc. The products sold in the newly liberalized economies of the world are generally those of big multinationals, such as Philips, Nestle, Ford, Sheraton, Visa, etc. Whether in Nairobi, Mumbai, Karachi, Buenos Aires, Kathmandu, Jakarta or New Delhi, the power of this advertising-based, global, mass-market, data-driven culture is steadily on the rise. Although sometimes 'dubbed' in local languages, the content of this homogenization varies from nation to nation.

The new ruling class in the new homogenized public will be concentrated in nations in the northern hemisphere, but its members will also be found in Mumbai, Bangalore, Delhi, Chennai, Kolkata and other major cities of India. They move from continent to continent, communicate instantaneously in English. They have immediate access to implausibly comprehensive networks of information, making financial transactions in Hong Kong, Sydney, London, Singapore, Kolkata or somewhere else, and they swap over scientific information, weather conditions, business news, reports and political engagement at the touch of a device. They constitute the public screen of India.

The political, economic and military dominance and success of the US, in the post-war period, were probably largely due to the Americanization of pop culture across the world. At the same time, the rarely defined and clarified process of Americanization is often held as accountable for the growing homogenization, hybridization and interdependence of cultures across the world. In the views of many proponents of western nations, the close link to the metropolitan America has also been the motivating reason for erosion of cultural multiplicity, political differences and sovereignty.

Intelligent machines, in particular, have registered new forms of social space in which the things that are American—from education to politics to war—have been reinforced in the Indian society. Now, a new techno-colonial world has emerged where we frequently are vulnerable to alien identities and values.

In the coming years, the entire world will be effectively controlled by a small group of individuals. They can be recognized handily by a few simple characteristics: those who have computer literacy, know how to use intelligent technologies, have Internet access and personalized communication channels such as websites and cell phones, and those who comprehend, speak and write English as their first, second or third language. At the centre of this remains data—those who possess data and those who create it by way of using intelligent technologies.

# 16

## Data at Risk

Popular Chinese-owned video-sharing social media platform, TikTok, has been fined $5.7 million by the US government on February 2019 for illegally collecting personal data of children.[130] In 2018, Twitter was investigated by Irish privacy authorities over its refusal to give information about how it tracks users. When Twitter users put links into tweets, the service applies its own link-shortening service (t.co). Privacy researchers suspected that Twitter gets more information when people click on links in this domain. Twitter might be using the shortening service to track people by leaving cookies in their browsers.[131]

Google has been fined $57 million by the French data protection authority, CNIL. Google broke the European Union's General Data Protection Regulation (GDPR), which came into effect in May 2018. When users give in to 'consenting', they are allowing Google to use personal information for advertising purposes when setting up new accounts. But the problem is that the information users were given beforehand was much too fragmented and vague for them to understand precisely what they were consenting to.[132] Google faced a $22.5 million fine by the US Federal Trade Commission (FTC) for breaching the privacy of iPhone and iPad users. Flouting the cookie rejection settings on the devices, Google managed to access the privacy of users, say reports.[133]

More than 20 child protection, consumer and privacy groups alleged that YouTube is violating the Children's Online Privacy

Protection Act (COPPA) and collects data from underage users, using that data to push advertisements to them.[134]

Amazon employees, particularly in China, were alleged to have been selling user information and other confidential material to independent sellers. They are also said to have been offering to delete negative reviews and restore banned accounts in exchange for a bribe[135] and it suffered a data breach, disclosing the names and email addresses of a number of its users.[136]

UK's Information Commissioner's Office (ICO) and its data protection authority in the Netherlands both announced a decision to fine Uber for disclosure delay. The UK fine amounted to £385,000 and the fine from the Netherlands amounted to €600,000. In all, the breach impacted some 2.7 million users in the UK and nearly 200,000 in the Netherlands.[137]

In the same way, Facebook faced a data breach under a privacy watchdog in the European Union which could fine Facebook as much as $1.63 billion. The case involved hackers compromising the accounts of more than 50 million users.

In 2013–14, Yahoo had breached 3 billion user accounts; it represented the largest data breach in history. In 2014, eBay had discovered a data breach that impacted 145 million eBay users. Equifax, in one of the largest cyber attacks of 2017, found that the personal information of 143 million consumers had been compromised and an additional 209,000 also had their credit card data exposed.[138]

Look at the various reports of fines and allegations framed against tech giants. The common thread that united all the aforesaid incidents is data breach. This sort of data breach got into wider public attention very recently as Cambridge Analytica was said to be involved in the data leak of 50 million Facebook users.

## Cambridge Analytica

Cambridge Analytica (CA), a British political consulting firm, with offices in London, New York City and Washington, D.C., began operations in 2013 as an offshoot of the Strategic Communications Laboratories (SCL) group founded by the conservatives Steve Bannon and American hedge-fund manager, Robert Mercer. It specializes in what is called psychographic profiling, which deals with attitudes, interests, personality, values, opinions and lifestyle. For example, purchasing priorities, medical history, automobile preferences, travel priorities, clothing styles, food habits, books one searches on Amazon, sexual orientation, political views, ideological lenience—almost all human behaviour was thought to be predicted using psychographics.

CA faced questions over whether it used personal data to influence the outcome of the US presidential election in 2016 and the Brexit referendum in the UK. However, the CA story doesn't end there, since its website boasts that the firm had supported more than 100 campaigns across five continents.[139] A Channel 4 investigation reported that CA and its parent company SCL had worked in more than 200 elections across the world, including the Czech Republic, Ukraine, Kenya, Nigeria, Mexico, Colombia and Brazil. CA itself had collaborated with the organization Pig.gi in Mexico and Ponte Esragia in Brazil, just to name a few.[140]

In 2014, a quiz on Facebook invited users to find out their personality type. It was developed by University of Cambridge academic Aleksandr Kogan. The app name was This Is Your Digital Life, which was designed to harvest not only the user data of the person taking part in the quiz, but also the data of their friends.[141]

Christopher Wylie, the whistle-blower, who worked with CA, alleged that since 270,000 people took part in the quiz and downloaded the app, the profile data of some 50 million users, mainly in the US, was harvested without their explicit consent. Wylie claimed the data was sold to CA, which then used it to psychologically profile people and deliver pro-Donald Trump content to them, by which the firm engaged with mind-control activities.[142] The other key point was that even the people who directly took part in the personality quiz had no idea that they were potentially sharing their data with Donald Trump's election campaign.

Different from the previous estimate of more than 50 million, Mark Zuckerberg, the CEO of Facebook, on 4 April 2018 said that the personal information of up to 87 million users, mostly in the US, may have been improperly shared with political consultancy CA.[143]

Previous to this, little thought had been given to the impacts of data in the social world. However, the idea that data buttress immense potentialities in the marketing world was so trendy. As the CA episode became public talk, other issues of data harvesting arrived in public discussion and the #deletefacebook movement started trending.

When users were deleting their Facebook accounts following the scandal of CA, they found that these social networking sites now held more details about their personal lives than they had expected.

Facebook makes it hard for users to delete their accounts. Instead, it pushes users to deactivate their account, leaving all personal data on Facebook's servers. When users again ask the company to permanently delete their accounts, the company suggests this: 'You may want to download a copy of your info from Facebook.' This data dump has indeed revealed the magnitude of data harvesting by Facebook.

## The Indian Concerns

In the West, data protection has enormous implications. In India, data protection standards are not as established as those in the western world. Let us see the issues involved.

Facebook on 4 April 2018 announced that 335 people in India had directly been affected through the installation of the app This Is Your Digital Life, and another 562,120 people were potentially affected as Facebook friends of those users who downloaded it. The figure of 562,455 was 0.6 per cent of the global number of potentially affected people. But the episode raised questions why CA accessed the user data of over 5 lakh people in India. The first implication is that whether CA got clients in India. Congress and BJP accused each other of using the services of third parties. Christopher Wylie has claimed that the data analytics firm worked extensively in India. He believed that the Congress party employed the firm for certain regional elections in India. Wylie's statement was a part of his testimony before the British Parliament's Digital, Culture, Media and Sports Committee, which was investigating the issue of the Facebook data breach.[144]

When probed by Labour MP Paul Farrelly about CA's role in India, Wylie said that the firm has offices and employees in the country, and he offered to produce documents related to the firm's operation in India. This revelation confirmed that data harvesting had reached India.[145]

## NaMo App

The political battle in India has shifted to a new political theatre following the CA disclosure: smart apps. There was an allegation that the NaMo app had leaked the user details of those who downloaded it.[146] The issue was that whether such user data was leaked or retrieved with the permission of those who downloaded it. Was the data from NaMo sourced to a third party violating user privacy?

The US-based start-up CleverTap, founded by three Indians, is facing the heat after a pseudonymous researcher alleged that the NaMo app was sourcing personal information like name, email, mobile number, device information and location to servers controlled by the start-up without the users' explicit approval.[147] The allegation was raised by the Congress party, based on the Tweets of a French researcher who goes by the pseudonym Elliot Alderson (a character from the Netflix show Mr Robot).[148]

Several reports have identified the man behind the Twitter profile as Robert Baptiste, a 28-year-old French security researcher and telecommunications engineer. He had also found 'something interesting' in the Congress's membership app, too, which was later removed.[149]

## Aadhaar

The Government of India was grappling with questions on protecting citizen information. Aadhaar, a 12-digit unique identification number issued to all Indian citizens based on their biometric and demographic data, was subjected to a data breach scandal in 2017.[150] The data is collected by the Unique Identification Authority of India (UIDAI), a statutory authority established in January 2009 by the Government of India, under the jurisdiction of the Ministry of Electronics and Information Technology, following the provisions of the Aadhaar (Targeted Delivery of Financial and Other Subsidies, Benefits and Services) Act 2016. Privacy campaigners are worried about attempts to link this 12-digit unique identity number with other identifications, such as bank accounts, passport, PAN cards, mobile phone numbers and income tax.

A report in the newspaper *The Tribune* exposed that you can access details to any Aadhaar holder's data repository just by making a payment of ₹500 through an unspecified service on WhatsApp.[151] So you enter an Aadhaar number into the system. It will reveal the holder's information, including date of birth, photo, phone number, name, address, PIN, e-mail, etc. About one billion Aadhaar holders' details can be accessed this way, claims the report. The report alleged that a further payment of ₹300 allowed printing of an Aadhaar card. The UIDAI denied the accusation in its response to this report. It stated that there was no data breach and that the biometric data was secure.[152]

Data is the legacy of the new century and the sublime resource of the twenty-first century, akin to oil in the last quarter of the twentieth century. Human life is data-driven in the new century. Data-driven human lives are stored and archived in retrieval form at multiple levels, which can be accessed, whenever required, by corporates, national governments or any others who need it for multiple reasons. For that matter, data is money. Data is cultural power, and whosoever possesses it will colonize others.

# 17

# We Have Something to Hide

We know when someone is observing us, and that is okay. But what if someone is observing us without our knowledge? Surveillance is just that—done clandestinely and on behalf of some authority. As it is done without permission, it makes you feel uncomfortable and hostile, as it becomes a question of control and power. Simply put, surveillance is the observation and/or monitoring of a person. It is about systematic attention to personal data for the purposes of influencing people.[153]

As we have seen in previous chapters, all our data is available online. The development of new-age technologies has increased the ability to track, observe and monitor us. It will be looking into more and more previously private activities. Moreover, surveillance has implications beyond non-consensual State observation. Private surveillance is extremely powerful, and people increasingly consent to it and even participate in it. Economic incentives lead consumers to agree to installing surveillance devices in their personal technologies, be it their smartphone or car.[154]

## PRISM and Questions of Privacy

When so many of our actions are observable, searchable, recordable and traceable, close surveillance is much more intrusive than it was in the past. Edward Snowden's revelations about the NSA surveillance programme, called PRISM, a clandestine antiterrorism, mass-electronic surveillance, data-mining programme launched in 2007, is a case in point. Potential third parties could trace user identities, which are stored in a little over 180 information hubs in different parts of the cables in the USA.[155] NSA's British equivalent, Government Communications Headquarters (GCHQ) participated in it. NSA contractor Edward Snowden, who leaked its existence, warned that the extent of mass-data collection was far greater than what the public knew it to be. He termed it as a dangerous and criminal activity.[156]

Nine major American tech companies were reported to have given the NSA 'direct access' to their servers, under the data-collection programme PRISM. The charge was that the NSA and the FBI hooked directly into their central servers. They were extracting photographs, audio and video chats, documents, emails and connection logs that would enable analysts in tracking. Microsoft, Yahoo, Google, Facebook, Paltalk, AOL, Skype, YouTube and Apple were the corporates involved.[157]

The top-secret PRISM programme allowed the US intelligence community to gain access to a wide range of digital information. It included emails and stored data on foreign targets operating outside the US. The programme was court-approved, but did not seek individual permissions. Instead, it operated under a broader authorization from federal judges who oversaw the use of the Foreign Intelligence Surveillance Act (FISA).[158] The PRISM programme raised very serious questions. They are also vital, pertaining to privacy, secrecy and the protection of identity, in the Internet age.

For the US, surveillance is its strategy as part of a global mission. It is a power game, a question of dominance and hegemony. The point is that what made the NSA—thereby USA—more powerful is the Internet. There is a global grid of fibre-optic cables that now connects 40 per cent of all humanity.[159] The US is capable of both blanketing the globe and targeting specific individuals. It assembled the requisite technological tool-kit, specifically, access points to collect data, computer codes to break encryption, [160] data farms to store its massive digital harvest[161] and supercomputers for nanosecond processing of what it was engorging for itself.

By 2012, the centralization via digitization of all audio, video, textual and financial communications into a worldwide network of fibre-optic cables, allowed the NSA to monitor the globe by penetrating just 190 data hubs.[162] It is an extraordinary economy of force, for both political surveillance and cyber warfare. In a top-secret document dated 2012, the NSA shows the 'Five Eyes' allies (Australia, Canada, New Zealand, the UK and the US) and its 190 'access programmes' for penetrating the Internet's global grid of fibre-optic cables, for both surveillance and cyber warfare.[163]

## Surveillance in India

Surveillance has been rampant in recent years in India. Software Freedom Law Centre (SFLC) published a report titled 'India's Surveillance State'. It elaborates that various legislations in India, both central and state, give permissions to governments to intercept and monitor the nation's communication networks.[164]

An unknown number of Lawful Interception and Monitoring (LIM) systems, tasked with the collection and analysis of citizens' communications data and metadata, are already installed into India's communication networks. There are many such institutions in India, such as Central Monitoring System (CMS), Network Traffic Analysis (NETRA) and National Intelligence Grid (NATGRID). They all reveal the government's all-encompassing surveillance capabilities, which without the assurance of a matching legal and procedural framework to protect privacy, would threaten to be as intrusive as the US government's controversial PRISM project.

CMS was set up by C-DoT, an obscure government enterprise located on the outskirts of New Delhi. It has many capabilities, all related to surveillance. It can monitor and deliver Intercept Relating Information (IRI) across 900 million mobile (GSM and CDMA) and fixed (PSTN) lines as well as 160 million Internet users.[165] The report further makes many revelations. Currently, two government spy agencies—the Intelligence Bureau (IB) and the Research and Analysis Wing (RAW)—access citizens' data. Some other enforcement agencies will also have access to this data. The Central Bureau of Investigation (CBI), the Narcotics Control Bureau (NCB), the Directorate of Revenue Intelligence (DRI), the National Intelligence Agency (NIA), the Central Board of Direct Taxes (CBDT), the Military Intelligence (MI) and the home ministry are authorized to observe citizen data. They are authorized to intercept and monitor citizens' calls and emails, under the guidelines laid down by the Supreme Court, the Indian Telegraph Act 1985, Rule 419(A) and other related legislations.[166]

Surveillance is being globalized. India is part of this globalization effort of surveillance by way of investing massively on surveillance regimes. NATGRID gives 11 security agencies real-time access to 21 citizen databases to track information.[167] Some of the biggest and most notorious surveillance technology companies in the world, such as ZTE, Utimaco and Verint, operate offices in India.[168] The fact is that India's surveillance industry is also growing for the last couple of years. Kommlabs Dezign, Vehere, Paladion Networks, Clear Trail Technologies are Indian companies selling surveillance equipment.

## We Have Something to Hide

Most of us don't really know why surveillance is a bad idea and why we should be aware of it. We think that as it has something to do with privacy, we must be wary of it. We lack insight into what privacy means in this context. We know little of why it matters on the Internet. We have been living with this state of affairs largely because the threat of surveillance has been relegated to the domains of science fiction and failed totalitarian states. However, these prophecies are no longer science fiction. Our government has shown a keen interest in acquiring all our data and using it for unknown purposes.

Even though we have laws that protect us against government surveillance, clandestine government scrutiny cannot be questioned until it is uncovered. And even when it is exposed, our law of surveillance provides only minimal protection. Courts frequently dismiss challenges to such programmes for lack of substance, under the theory that mere surveillance causes no harm. However, the striking point is that we are lacking a critical insight into why (and when) government surveillance is dangerous. The prevailing attempts to track the dangers of surveillance are often unpromising. They generally fail to speak in ways that likely influence the law.

On one side, we think that surveillance is creepy. It is Orwellian and corrosive of civil liberties. On the other side, we believe that it keeps us safe. It makes our lives more convenient and gives us the benefit of free Internet. Moreover, some commentators argue that data surveillance does not affect privacy at all. Surveillance is thus confusing. We like its benefits, though we are fearful and sometimes dismissive of its costs. This confusion points to a larger problem.

The point is that civil liberty advocates lack a compelling account of when and why surveillance is harmful. Of course, we have a spontaneous understanding that public and private surveillance is potentially bad. While holding such a view, we do not have an articulate explanation of why it is bad. Some of our understanding comes from literature, such as George Orwell's chilling portrait of Big Brother in *1984*.

Advocates of surveillance will tell you that if you have not done anything wrong, you have nothing to fear. Indeed, it is a typical argument used by governments and other groups to justify their undercover activities. Significantly, surveillance will not target law-abiding citizens. If done so, it will not affect their lives. Instead, it will be making their lives more comfortable and safer, through the elimination of criminals. Thus, the government's use of various surveillance apparatus, such as camera surveillance in public places, warrantless phone tapping and Internet inspections, have the potential to save citizens' lives from criminals and terrorists. While doing so, there will only be minimal invasion of its citizens' privacy.

Surveillance proponents even ask all citizens to carry surveillance equipment, such as location-tracking devices. It would make the tracing of criminal acts much easier. Thus, it is easily argued that people refusing to carry these devices do so only because they have something to hide.

The counterargument is that it is not because people want to commit any crime or have something to hide that surveillance is objectionable, but because the methods are invasive and prone to abuse. Considering that, given current technologies, the government already has the ability to track us to a reasonable degree. It also has easy access to information, such as purchasing habits, phone conversations, online activities and emails. The case then, is that current surveillance practices are extreme and equally unacceptable.

This argument also fails to take into consideration a number of important issues. Collection of personally identifying data or recording them is vulnerable to abuse by trusted insiders. In addition, allowing secret surveillance, though in minor form and limited in scope, encourages the government to expand such surveillance programmes in the future. Aadhaar, in India, is an example. Reporter Rachna Khaira reported in *The Tribune* that anonymous sellers over WhatsApp were allegedly providing access to Aadhaar numbers for a fee of ₹500 and 10 minutes would give access to another one billion details.[169]

Different groups define appropriate limits for surveillance in different manners. One viewpoint that is found most interesting is that of MIT professor Gary Marx, who argued that before implementing surveillance, we should evaluate the proposed methods by asking a number of questions. The point is that the context, purposes, uses, etc. are important in surveillance systems. Such questions are important in the Internet age.[170]

Caspar Bowden, a privacy advocate, has rightfully stated that the rhetoric of having nothing to hide unless one is a criminal is fundamentally erroneous and unfounded. The problem is the idea that you have nothing to hide if you are not a criminal or terrorist, so surveillance need not be feared. The main problem is that if you are told 'you hide nothing, so you need not fear' is a doctrinal weapon used mostly by authoritarian establishments and society. These societies adopt a more paternalistic attitude. We need to make our leaders responsible to accord subjective value to the notion of privacy.[171] Jacob Applebaum, an American independent journalist and computer security researcher says that this rhetoric is merely a psychological coping mechanism when dealing with security.[172]

AI technology provides the government and big corporations massive capabilities for mass surveillance. It is dangerous because it enables discrimination based on almost all factors. Race, ethnic identity, religion, class, political beliefs—our vulnerabilities to discrimination by scrutiny is enormous. Surveillance is used to control what we can do, what we say, what we see and, ultimately, what we think. We cannot restrain it with any meaningful checks and balances. It makes us less safe. It makes us less free.

Privacy is an essential human need and central to our ability to control how we relate to the world. Being stripped of privacy is fundamentally dehumanizing and it makes no difference whether the surveillance is conducted by an undercover policeman following us around or by a computer algorithm tracking our every move. The rules we had enacted to protect us from these dangers under earlier technological laws are now woefully insufficient. They are not working; we need to fix that and we need to do it very soon.

# 18

# Our Lives as Marionettes

As we have seen, we frequently visit our social media profiles and upload information about ourselves—our holiday destinations, hotels we stayed in, cities we visited, products we bought, books we read, our political ideology, clothes and perfumes we wear, and the mobile brands we use to access networks!

We are aware that tech giants have algorithms that can predict behaviour. Machine learning system on search engines can predict what you would search, your preferences and what you like and dislike. This also means that the algorithm can predict your political orientation, your reading habits, your accommodation preferences, etc. Such data is extremely useful to corporates and other big players, such as political actors and online book stores. Almost all brands want insights into customer preferences, and this data helps towards that end.

Data is what makes decisions apt, correct and useful for the further growth of business. The billions of users of social media create huge volumes of unstructured data that is nearly impossible to process with standard statistical software applications. This is where big data analytics comes in.

Big data analytics make sense of the unstructured data and help to organize it into a more structured model to support business-based queries. Due to the massive size of social media data generated, brands are increasingly recognizing the importance of investing in analytics capabilities: to understand their customers better, to identify growth opportunities and to stay ahead of the competition. Imagine, this content you uploaded is used for purposes for which it was not meant to be!

Plenty of user activities are stored in Google's data archives. Facebook algorithms arrange a huge stockpile of user data in which great insights can be drawn up for brand marketing. For example, a global tour operator wants to know which tour locations are trending on Facebook. For this, image recognition software on Facebook can analyse it on its algorithm and identify what is trending, so that the tour operator can take decisions. Uber and other cab operators want to know cities you might visit, and subsequently can rank the cities according to travel priorities and frequency. In a similar way, brands related to clothes, mobiles, books, automobiles, household equipment, etc. can approach data vendors—thereby enabling data giants to implement business decisions.

This situation may sound like science fiction, in which robotics and AI are constantly observing humans. But this is our current reality. The algorithms upon which data giants provide you information easily tracks what is on your mind, as we can see when ads appear for things we search online. When you think of social media analytics, you might think about figures, graphs, illustrations and charts. You may have heard something about metrics, dashboards and data, sometimes data mining and data harvesting. If you are connected to the tech world, you may have heard of big data. And that would be accurate. Those are all important elements of using analytics. But that is far from the whole picture.

### The Tip of the Iceberg

So what really does happen with social media analytics? It is simple: business and profit—then thought control! Today, analytics can be applied to almost every field in the social world, let alone business. Election prediction has been traditionally done on numerical analysis, for example. Outside of election analysis, data-driven approaches have been applied to other fields, such as business, opinion-making, publicity and marketing.

But there is a limit to what numbers and data can accomplish. Money can't buy you happiness and numbers can't tell you what to care about. Sometimes, we can even get blinded by numbers. But with analytics, it's different: you can move from analytics to action if you have the know-how. Analytics, in a way, is like an iceberg. Most people only see the tip above the surface. In fact, most of the iceberg is hidden underwater. In the same way, most people associate analytics solely with what they can easily see above the surface, including actions that show up as numbers, graphs and reports.

Some of us might think that social media analytics is simply about the number of retweets on Twitter, fans on Facebook, views on YouTube or likes on Instagram. When you see these likes and tweets in numbers and graphs, it's easy to think, 'Yes, that is all there is to social media analytics.' But that is only the tip of the iceberg.

Social media analytics get their power from the foundation, where the bulk of the system is built layer upon layer. It's the area least subjected to constant change and erosion. It's also the portion least seen and understood. Most of the social media analytics system is hidden from the view of the people who see the results. Let's take a peek below the surface.

## Social Media Analytics: How Does It Work?

Social media analytics is the art and science of extracting insights from a vast amount of semi-structured and unstructured social media data. Those numbers about tweets, likes and other metrics are the key to our inner mind. That gives a clue to what we are thinking. Our interests and dislikes are embedded in those numbers. It is an art of interpreting and aligning the insights gained with goals and objectives.

Almost all social media platforms were created with a specific purpose. All of them had a specific set of users in mind. However, when we look back, none of them are acting solely upon the purpose for which it was created. For example, Instagram is supposed to be a platform where you can post all your pictures that tell the world around you and the latest happenings in your life. Is it just functioning along that line now? The answer is a big no. Politicians are using it to appeal to electors. Brands are using it to increase brand visibility. Famous people use it to build their popularity. In the same way, almost all social media platforms have transformed into a marketplace where web users are seen as products. Facebook is a powerful tool to influence people. WhatsApp is to communicate with people in a way that can even mislead and control you. Somebody needs our attention on these platforms. They want to build their visibility out there. Hence, social media analytics.

## Types of Analysis

There can be plenty of data analytics types. Geospatial analysis focusses on the location data of customers. Sentiment analysis investigates people's sentiments in a given situation. Influence analysis understands where a brand got influence within a social sphere. Machine data analysis is information that is produced by computer systems as processes or functions are executed. This machine data can provide the behavioural insights of a social media user, helping to create a view of what content they are interested in, how long they interact with information, or what advertisement they react to. Demographic analysis is important for brands. Some solutions utilize available data via feedback logs from the social networking platforms supplying the data, whereas others go beyond to leverage NLP technology to determine demographic details based on content and linguistic analysis.

Information on gender, age and ethnicity creates added value on social data. When this is available for analysis, it is possible to build highly detailed master data about customers who are socially active. Brand affinity is a metric to measure the goodwill created for branded products. For many marketing professionals, brand affinity analytics is a foundational function for building strategies.

Text analytics is a capability that gains insight from the output of NLP. Once the unstructured social media data has been collected and organized, text mining solutions can analyse the information to identify patterns and trends within the data. Text analytics is not different from data mining. It tries to organize the data for analysis. Once organized, it can produce insights otherwise too difficult for people to do by hand. Text analytics opens the door for innovative analysis of social media data.

## What Information Is Being Tracked?

Along with the different types of analysis that can be done on the collected data, social media platforms themselves offer analytics to users. Engagement is one of the most important measures of social media platforms, because it shows if people are interacting with your posts. The number of people who see your activities on their timelines and the number of users who saw the post is called 'impression'. The number of people who like your page and see your posts on their timelines, the number of times people hovered over your page name or profile picture to view your content on

Facebook, and the number of times your profile page has been viewed all fall under this umbrella.

Facebook Insights is free to all business pages. It's designed to help you understand your audience and how they interact with your posts. Twitter Analytics is a free programme available to every Twitter account that analyses your tweets and followers.

Facebook and Twitter are not the only platforms providing opportunities for marketing business plans. Snapchat, LinkedIn, Instagram, Pinterest and YouTube all have their own free benefits.

Snapchat started supplying data to content creators under Insights. You can now see the total story views by week, month and year; time spent viewing stories in minutes; daily unique story viewers; and some audience demographics and interests. Business profiles on Instagram have access to Instagram Insights. There, you can view impressions, reach and profile visits. You can also see what times of the day your followers engage with your profile, which can help you determine the time when you should post new content.

You also need a business-specific account for Pinterest Analytics. This tells you what pins people like and what they save from your website, and from there, you can learn what your customers really want. A company's LinkedIn page administrator can see engagement with individual posts, follower demographics, comments, shares and the number of new followers. You can also monitor the performance of your YouTube videos, measuring where the traffic is coming from, how long people watch videos, how many people watch a specific video and some other demographics. The filters possible for this data include content, device type, geography, date or timeframe, all video, subscriber status, live versus on-demand playback, translation use, and traffic by video.

## The New Purpose of Social Media

What do all the measurement and analytics types tell us? Simple, that these social media platforms have transformed from their earlier roles of connection to a new scenario in which the connection is linked to the market. Our activities on their platform are considered products. Value creation on social media is what a business model looks for. Social media data is considered the new gold in the twenty-first century. Corporates leverage the vast amount of social-media data to start identifying which customer behaviours and actions create more value. With increasing data and more sophisticated social media analytics, companies need to tap into the vast amounts of data produced by social media users to increase brand loyalty, generate leads, drive traffic, make forecasts and ultimately make the right business decisions. Social media data and users are of significant value to businesses. Now, we are controlled by these brand builders on social media. We are their products.

The backbone of analytics is crowd-sourcing algorithms, such as recommendation engines, social bots and cookies. A 2017 estimate suggested that 23 million bots operate on Twitter, whereas 140 million on Facebook and 27 million on Instagram.[173] Humans need not tell them what to do. They simulate the behaviour of human beings in a social media environment. Interacting with other users, they share information and messages.[174] On social media, bots are capable of several social interactions. These make them appear to be a regular human-like person. They respond to postings. They respond to questions from other users. They can search for influential users on a particular social-media platform. For instance, they look for Twitter and Facebook users who have lots of followers. Bots learn from how people use social media sites, how often they visit a particular website and which pattern of information and content people like the most.[175]

Cookies on the computer or mobile systems track user actions on the Internet across all the websites one has visited. Cookies, once agreed to, save, and even store, cookies from websites that the users haven't logged on. One may call these third-party cookies. Then there arises a problem. These cookies, saved from websites one has never visited, report that your browser has visited them. That also means some third parties have collected data about you without your permission. You can also call these cookies as tracking cookies—or trackers for short.

Trackers come from companies that collect and analyse your web usage to personalize ads. Take the case of Facebook. Many web platforms embed Facebook's like button on their website. Why? Facebook has a data-sharing arrangement with other websites. Both share details about your habits, attitudes, preferences, interests and dislikes through this data sharing arrangement. Every time you visit a website, it reports to Facebook that you have visited them. This happens even if you don't press the like button on the website you visited. It also happens whether or not you logged into Facebook. It doesn't even matter whether you are a Facebook user or you have a Facebook account at all. What is the advantage for the owners of the website? The particular website can have a wider audience. Besides, the website can also look at reports of Facebook about who visited its website.[176] And it can arrange deals with Facebook to show ads in the newsfeed of users.

Facebook, Google and other big-data platforms provide trackers to analyse the websites you have visited. They profile what you did while you are on a website. They gather information about what other pages you open, what links you click and how much time you spend there. They can analyse this information by running scripts on your web browser. You may not be even aware of it.[177] The websites you visit and your actions on those websites give valuable information about you to the social media-analytics firms. They use this information to calculate models to predict your buying behaviour. The firms that collect these personality profiles sell their products through micro-targeting. They select and deliver the kinds of advertisements you are most likely to react positively to. Maybe you are unaware that Facebook sells ads to companies for selling products like the ones you looked at on other websites. Maybe you are unaware that Google and other bigger data giants have data-sharing agreements with websites through which they show you ads to sell products. Have you ever looked at shoes on a shoe-selling website, cars at car-selling websites and costumes at a fashion website? Then, the next time on you are on YouTube, Google or Facebook, do you notice that they are showing the same ads? That is how cookies work.

One important concern here is about the purpose for which the data from social media goes for functions. Not everyone is in the business of cookies and tracking for promoting household or harmless products. Some social media-analytics firms don't want to sell you a product like a car, smartphone or a book. What if some firms specialize in analysing your data to convince you to vote for a political candidate? What if a firm that specializes in analysing data about you engages in impression management? What if a firm specializes in analysing data to indoctrinate people ideologically and selectively share news to your newsfeed on Facebook and Twitter? And it is not a hypothetical situation. There are firms which specialize in how to 'push your buttons' to persuade you to vote for one candidate or political party, and another based on socio political issues. There are firms that specialize in creating perspectives.

It is a dangerous blend of technology and ideology. Once you respond to these stories or comment on them, the data about your preferences becomes even more refined. The social media platforms don't decide what to show you. However, they get the profile of your preferences and associations. They sell access to people like you to the advertisers and their messages come to you, automatically, using the social media platform.[178] The evolving social media universe has far-reaching impacts on our social living. Relationship, opinion-making, buying and selling, and other human behaviours are going to be shaped by the people behind this type of analytics.

I have bought books, phones and other household items based on what my social media friends had posted. All of us have had purchasing decisions because of the stuff that has come across our social media feeds. The point is that what we do on social media is not just entertainment. Our activities out there influence the purchasing decisions of many other people, just as we make decisions by seeing what our friends posted there. Social media has transformed into a bigger ad campaign where we are already being targeted by big corporates.

So, the next time you engage in any kind of activity on social media, think twice because what you are doing for your own mental pleasure is a product for somebody completely unknown to you. What makes you a product? Just your retweets, links shared, photos updated, the comments dropped on some other individual's social media posts, YouTube views, video uploads and everything else. Very sensitive personal data, including your most intimate information are tracked for analytics. Beware, you are a product on social media!

# 19

# Social Contract: Violated?

Internet giants like Twitter and Facebook offer a business model which persuades its users to share as much personal information as possible. It is on this data you have created on their platform that these data firms make their profit. The greater the data you give them, more is their industry visibility and profits. Data is intangible. We don't know what data we have created. It is a by-product of our online activity as well as the use of digital technology. For us, it is easy to ignore or forget about it. Hence most of data harvesting is invisible to us.

### Where Else Are We Creating Data?

Your word processor keeps a record of what you have written, where you write and revise documents, including your drafts and changes. It also maintains a record of who created the document and who else worked on it by using cookies installed on your device.[179]

Your cell phone is continuously calculating its location based on which cell tower is nearest. It is not because your phone company particularly cares where you are, but it needs to know where your cell phone is in order to route telephone calls to you. Of course, when you actually use that phone, you produce more data, such as numbers dialled, calls received, text messages sent and received and call duration. If it is a smartphone, it is also a computer, and all your apps produce data when you use them and sometimes even when you are not using them. Your smartphone probably has a GPS receiver, which produces even more accurate location information than the cell tower. The GPS receiver in your smartphone provides you location within 16–27 feet, while cell towers to about 2,000 feet.

When you are buying something from a store, you are creating more data. The store has a cash register, which is a computer and keeps a record of the time and date of what you purchased. If your payment is an online transaction, the banking details, including your credit card or debit card particulars, tied to that purchase remain tracked. Data is also sent to the credit card company and at times, some of it comes back to you in your monthly bill. A video camera is installed in the store to record evidence in case of a theft or fraud, and another camera is recording you when you use an ATM. There are more cameras installed outside, monitoring buildings, roadways, sidewalks and other public places.

Get into a car and you generate even more data. Modern cars are loaded with computers. It creates data on speed, how hard you are pressing on the pedals, what position the steering wheel is in and more. The data so generated is automatically recorded in a recorder, useful for figuring out what happened in an accident or sporadic service. There is even a computer in each tyre, gathering pressure data.

If you use a fitness tracking device like Fitbit or Jawbone, it helps you collect information about your wake and sleep schedules and movements, and uses that to analyse both your exercise and sleep habits. It can determine when you are having sex. Give the device more information about yourself, how much you weigh, what you eat and so on—then it can learn even more about you.

The fact that the price of DNA sequencing continues to drop has a reason. Most of us are signing up to generate and analyse our own genetic data at no cost. Companies like 23andMe use genomic data from their customers to find genes associated with disease, leading to new and highly profitable cures. Insurance companies may someday buy your health data to make business decisions.

You can download life-logging apps that record your activities on your smartphones. Activities like talking to friends, playing games, watching movies and so on are recorded. But this is just the tip of the iceberg of what life-logging could become. It will include a video record of your details. Google Glass is the first wearable device that has this capability, but others are not far behind.

It wasn't always like this. In the era of radio, newspapers and television, we received information, but no record of the event was stored. Now, we get news and entertainment on the Internet. We used to speak to people face-to-face and then by telephone. Now, we have conversations over text or email. People used to buy things with cash at a store in the past. Now, credit cards over the Internet have replaced physical cash. We paid with coins at a tollbooth, subway or parking meter. Now, we use automatic payment systems such as FASTag that are connected to our licence plate number and credit card. Taxis used to be cash-only, until we started paying by credit card. Now, we are using our smartphones to access networked taxi systems like Uber and Ola, which produce data records of the transaction, along with our pick-up and drop-off locations.

## Our Pocket Surveillance Devices

If you need to be more convinced that you are living in a surveillance society where data about you is constantly being collected, look at your smartphone. This incredibly powerful device is so central to your life; indeed, it has become an extension of your physical body. It seems perfectly normal for people to pull this device out of their pocket, no matter where, and use it to connect with someone else, no matter where the other person is. But that device in your hand is not as simple as you think. So long as you carry it with you, many things you may think unimportant to you become important to forces totally unknown to you.

Every day, when you put your smartphone in your pocket, you are making an agreement with many forces. First of all, your device is manufactured by a firm. It requires an operating system. For example Apple's operating system, iOS, runs on the company's iPod, iPad, iPhone and Apple Watch devices. The Android OS is owned by Google, which is open-source, in contrast to Apple's closed system. Microsoft is no infant to computer operating systems; however, it is a relative newcomer to mobile operating systems. Blackberry's operating system was well-liked for its enhanced security and safety measures among a core group of customers.

You may use the device following an unwritten contract in which you say, 'I want to use my mobile; in exchange, I allow this company to know where I am and what I am doing at all times.' This tracking isn't defined in any agreement, but it is inherent in how the mobile operating system works for you. It doesn't end there.

Smartphones cannot be that great, and they can't work for you unless those mobile service providers know where you are, who you are and many other identifying information. It also means they keep you under their hidden surveillance. It is a very intimate form of surveillance. Through your smartphone, it tracks where you live and where you are employed. It tracks your weekend destinations and evening plans. It tracks how often you go to shrines and which shrines, how much time you spend in a shop and whether you speed when you drive. It learns about all the other phones in your area, so it is easy to track with whom you spend your days with, whom you meet for lunch and whom you sleep with.

The accumulated data can better picturize how you spend your time than you, because it doesn't have to rely on human memory. Before smartphones, if someone wanted to know all of this, they would have had to hire a private investigator or a spy to follow you around taking notes. That job is now obsolete. The smartphone in your hand does all of this without a human person's intervention. No one retrieves that information, but it is there for mining.

Your location information is decisive, and everyone wants to access it. The police wants it. Governments also use this same sort of data for intimidation and social control. Business outlets need it for brand advertisements targeted to you and many other entities. Companies such as Verint, Cobham, Defentek have developed tracking systems.

There is another more accurate location-tracking system built into the smartphone: GPS. It provides location data to the various apps running on your smartphone. Some apps in the smartphone use location-tracker data to deliver service: Google Maps, Yelp, Uber, etc. Others, like Angry Birds, collect and sell it for those who need it for purposes. Such surveillance methods are even accessible to us as users. For example, HelloSpy is an app that one can install on somebody's smartphone to track their activities. It is perfect for an anxious mom wanting to spy on her teenager or an abusive husband to spy on his wife. Employers have used these apps as well to spy on their employees.

## Surveillance Leads to Data Broking

There is a whole industry profiting from tracking you in real-time. For this industry, the more data you generate, the greater your value as a product. They collect and aggregate information from a wide range of sources to create detailed profiles of you. They sell or share your personal information with others, including businesses, government agencies, other individuals and data brokers. In some cases, they might exchange this information under a cooperative arrangement rather than sell it. In other instances, they might provide the information at no cost, making money through advertising. And all this is possible because of the constant surveillance we are under.

One of the important sources remains social media sites such as Facebook, YouTube, LinkedIn and Twitter. They collect a wide variety of data. Much of the information is demographic in nature and may include your names, addresses, telephone numbers, emails, age, gender, family status, marital status, number and ages of children, religion, data about real estate owned, political affiliation, income level, education and occupation.

Some data vendors collect lists of people experiencing life events such as having a baby, getting married, moving, buying a home, purchasing a car or getting divorced. Other data brokers collect more specialized types of information, including purchasing history, automobiles owned, social media history, hobbies and interests, medical conditions and payment methods used. All your information is practically compromised so that you have no data privacy.

Most of us don't realize the magnitude at which computers are integrated into everything we do. We know little of the fact that computer storage has become cheap enough to make it feasible to indefinitely save all the data we churn out. Most of us also underestimate just how easy it has become to identify us using data that we consider anonymous.

# 20

# We Are Data

As we have seen in the previous chapters, the race to obtain data is already on, as various data giants have adopted a business model of attention merchants. Under the guise of free information, services and entertainment, they capture our attention and obtain huge amounts of data about us and all our activities. Then, they resell this to advertisers and other clients. In this market, we aren't their customers, we are their products.

Data, which is collected and processed through surveillance, data theft and other ways is the means for this new appropriation of our intellectual labour, cognitive abilities and social life. The lack of ethical processes around collection, processing and management of data reduce our life to computational numerals.

Unlike markets of the previous epochs in history, intelligent technology is central to the data-based-attention economy. This huge significance of technology represents a historical shift from machines that serve us to intelligent machines that dominate our lives.

During the twenty-first century and beyond, technology is not to replace human labour and make life comfortable, but to replace humans itself. Tech giants have grown far from what they were originally thought to be. Google, which began as a search engine, has now transformed into Alphabet, and its portfolio encompasses several futuristic industries. Calico is investing in anti-ageing. GV seeks to invest in start-ups in life science, AI, agriculture and others. Verily focusses on ideas like surgical robots and contact lenses that allow people with diabetes to continually check their glucose levels. Waymo is a self-driving technology under development. X is a semi-secret research facility, which is to invent and launch 'moonshot' technologies that aim to make the world a radically better place. Project Glass would be the hands-free display of information that allows for interaction with the Internet via natural-language voice commands. Makani is designed to produce wind energy using kites. Project Loon brings Internet access to everyone by creating an Internet network of balloons. Project Wing aims to rapidly deliver products across a city by using flying vehicles.[180]

Most tech giants, such as Apple, Facebook, Uber, are investing in futuristic technologies. Therefore, online shopping will become digital, according to Amazon. Travel becomes digital, according to Uber. Food delivery becomes digital, according to Swiggy. Watching movies becomes digital, according to Netflix. These activities will be carried on by data. In all walks of our life, some tech giants shape our behaviour, control us and even shape our thoughts. What is central to these tech giants and their futuristic inventions is data! The greater the data they collect about us, the closer they are to our mind. Their technologies are entirely different from those of previous generations.

We generate enormous data. Data is huge, which the human brain alone cannot process. But the same data is our enemy, for it watches us. It exposes our privacy. Data analytics is being developed, which can delve deep into user activities. Using machine learning, now it is easy to predict human behaviour.

Predictive social algorithm is set to shape our behaviour. Forces unknown to us control us from remote locations. They can predict what we think, feel and overall know almost all our emotions. They can even predict when we have a feeling, because data giants shape our feelings! Filter bubbles reinforces one-sided thoughts and our thinking processes are thereby custom-generated.

## The Death of Personal Freedom?

For centuries, we believed that political authority came from divine laws rather than from the human heart. Only in the last few centuries has it been known that the source of authority comes from humans. Liberalism upheld free will and individual choice as supreme virtues. What we choose, says liberalism, is an outcome of our free will. Thomas Hobbes (1588–1679), a British philosopher, is believed to have said in the book *Leviathan* that humans have a will that is free.[181] The free mind gives signal to the body to act. Our physical activities are first imagined in the mind. But free will is going to be enslaved. Soon, our authority, which is a product of human free will, is going to shift from humans to algorithms. Big-data algorithms will undermine the very idea of human freedom.

In the days to come, what we choose, buy, like and love will be decided not by that moment—the cognitive moment or self-reflection. Technology will surpass our cognitive skills and predict our decisions and behaviour in advance. The books, car, food, clothes that you plan to buy or the courses you opt for for higher studies, the job you prefer, the relationships, sexual drive—all these behaviours will be predicted by AI and big-data analytics.

The future model of our society is data-driven, which is complex and replete with privacy issues. For that matter, data is money and is cultural power. Collecting, analysing, cleaning, processing and gaining useful insights from data is the new way to gain power.

## Digital Brains

Data multiplies every second. The velocity of events and information in the twenty-first century surpasses all previous epochs in human history. But the paltry human ability to process, archive and memorize the huge inventory of information is inadequate. The data age has already overtaken the human brain and our cognitive abilities. The twenty-first century exposed the inadequacy of the human brain to process huge data. Hence, we are in need of technology to help us do all the things that our brain has done for us. Information technology is our intimate friend, for it does all the functions of data processing—editing, storing and retrieval.

The problem with our present technology is that it cannot think for us. It delivers us the kind of information we want on demand. The information it provides is based on a script that humans have written. That is, we are using a platform to carry information from one point to another. We are already done with it in the beginning of the twenty-first century.

What we need is a new brain in the future. We are in need of technologies that think for us, predict and do all our activities. We can call our new brain AI. It is our new brain for the twenty-first century and even beyond. We have already surrendered to this new brain. Making sense of our new brain is the first thing we have to do to face our own future in the new century. AI works in a rather indeterminate way.

Our inner mind is conquered by intelligent machines. We can call it machine learning. They are monsters, even taller than our nation, which do not know that our cognitive mind is accessed by data firms. Data breach becomes the new normal.

As we increasingly distrust ourselves, in our place, there are human-like artificial, organic biological machines; they are our non-human friends. Thus, social robotics replaces many human-only skills.

## Data Imperialism

The political question of this transformation is data imperialism. Things that are American, from education to politics and war has been reinforced everywhere. We are reduced to data. Our value is reduced to some computational values. Like the oil economy, capitalism thrives on data. Data is going to colonize our life and appropriate it for the growth of capitalism. Technology has metamorphosed to the playground of a few big players like Google, Uber, Facebook, Twitter, YouTube, and just a handful of other big names.

Technology that enables tech giants and data firms to manipulate our attention is the new way of colonization. Bad actors exploit the design of technology to bring harm to us and even kill innocent people amongst us. Our democracy is undermined because of design choices and business decisions by data giants that deny responsibility for the consequences of their actions. The work culture of these companies causes employees to be indifferent to the negative side-effects of their firms' success.

Technology platforms, including Facebook and Google, are the beneficiaries of attention. They have taken advantage of our attention, using sophisticated techniques to prey on the weakest aspects of human psychology, to gather and exploit private data and to craft business models that do not protect users from harm. The data giants dominated the attention-economy revolution, thereby masking an unmitigated disaster for our democracy, for public health, for personal privacy and for the economy.

In the present day of the ubiquitous data-colonized world, who we are is not just what we think we are. Who we are is what our data is created to say about us. Everything is becoming data. Our social world is transforming into data with computational value. Relationships, emotions, pastime activities, parenting, healthcare, education, almost everything is reduced to just data. Your activities have value only if it is mined as data!

## Data Is Power

Data is power in the present century, which is potent enough to mould and alter social relationships. However, unlike previous centuries, the new power structure configured by data is barely traceable on the ground. Data has had a significant role in history. It isn't any phenomenon that originated in the contemporary world. Even great emperors of the past carried along with them cartographers and scholars to map, learn and contextualize the information about the lives and geographies of the alien lands which were newly conquered. Information was an important determinant of control.

The modern nation, originating in Europe, first conducted extensive census about the people and settlement so as to ensure a consistent revenue extraction and more. However, the nature of the collection of information became very different when these States in Europe colonized various parts of the world and created empires. The most visible example is India, where British colonizers conducted extensive census surveys covering the ethnic and cultural details, which was different from those they had conducted in their nation with their citizens. Information acted as an important conditioning to power, to control and stabilize the colonial rule by introducing new labels and categories of caste and community in the society. The purpose of collecting and managing data by the colonial state in India wasn't to protect the interest of stakeholders but, like any modern nation, to reinforce the sovereignty of the State power remained at the centre of all initiatives to collect data.

Every society progresses, or to be politically correct, moves ahead completely crumbling the existing order, and at times evolving new distinct changes by retaining certain elements of the preceding order. Societies move from a particular kind of social–economic–political–cultural organization to the other due to new changes in the society from technological innovations to popular revolutions. The development of history through various stages was importantly stressed by Karl Marx with his stages theory of historical progression, where history travelled from primitive communism to slave society to feudal society and to capitalism, which would then further into what he calls socialism. He understands the engine of change in each phase of history through the variable of class antagonism and variations in the means of production—the latter being the structural change and the former agentive change that pushes one society to a new world order. In every society, the design of economy, socio-cultural realm and political sphere are laid down within the existing matrix of power in the society. But what is giving rise to power is intriguing.

Power, being an important political concept, simply translates to the ability of eliciting the predicted reactions generally—but it is so much more. Rather than defining power, it would be better if one traverse briefly through various locations of power in history so as to have a comprehensive idea of power. In Ancient Greece, power resides in the polis, an administrative city centre, which is run by citizens. But what made the citizen acquire power was not his intellectual deliberative capacities and orientation towards the polis but the leisure citizens get for leading a life of contemplation, made possible by slaves who engaged in manual labour due to citizens. What makes someone a citizen then definitely depends on his ownership of slaves—making citizens acquire power. Following the history of the West, especially of western Europe, then one other important driver of power after slaves was landed property, wherein the landowners, feudal lords or aristocrats had amassed great wealth and power out of the tenants and land. They even collided with the political power, since the political realm was separate from the social and economic, the latter being designed by feudal lords. With the writings of John Locke, one of the important institutions that determine various relationships came into being: private property. The one who puts labour into natural resources can place a claim on the value-added resources as their property; society should recognize and the political order is bound to protect the claim. This is also followed by Adam Smith and David Ricardo, who proposed the labour theory of value and the free competition and flow of trade between countries that would result in social benefit. The location of power, here, seems to take the individualist level, where the creation of value through labour becomes an important source of power. That made individuals claim ownership.

With the Industrial Revolution and the reign of capitalism, the power of labour was replaced by machine power. Karl Marx calls the man's essential being as labouring, which is alienated from him. Under the capitalist regime, the owners of means of production—labour, machine, land and organization—became the centre of power. Workers started to become estranged from labour, nature, people and their product. Machinery, an important source of power, replaced labour power and made man the machines. However, this dominance of machines was replaced in what Daniel Bell calls 'post-industrial society', where knowledge and skill become a source of power. The service economy generates more wealth than the manufacturing-based economy. The economy that offers mainly services to people will give a natural goodbye to an economy that provides goods and products.

Now we are passing through a stage which, according to MIT professors Erik Brynjolfsson and Andrew McAfee, is 'the second machine age' in which machines replace human cognitive activities.[182] This stage is vital, as it replaces humans from everything possible to the maximum extent by what may be called quantification of life in which data become central to life.

Social relationships, economy, politics, culture—every single thing is potently affected by the new source of power: data. Data power is not a simple idea like how social power was exercised in different epochs in human history, say ownership of slave in ancient Greece, land owned in the feudal age, machineries and capital held in the industrial age, and the monopoly over oil in the twentieth century. Unlike previous societies where slave, land, machines, etc., which crumbled societies and eventually got liberated from, data as a source of power is not showing any optimism of bringing a rupture. Data power is based on invisible social relationships. It's existing in a state of flux.

## Data Is Our Labour

Data, which users create and forget for the reason that it's of no value from practical considerations in lieu of Google search behaviour and Facebook timelines to websites and video-sharing sites, is absolutely valuable from a provider's perspective. Hence, it's a product for a provider but of no significance from a user who creates the data. However, the data people create is strategically important for the future world, where their social life, metaphorically from birth to death, is shaped by those who own the data. Today, information gets reduced to quantifiable and scalable terms, which are data, and is now potent enough for predicting, rating and controlling the society. Data in the twenty-first century is highly complex from that of previous centuries.

One point must be emphasized: data is our labour. Huge data is left behind. Who owns this data is fundamental to power. Human beings are social and interacting animals. Going along a Marxist trajectory, if we consider our interactions as what we are, or as our labour, then one should definitely have a claim of its ownership. Our activities online pertain to us. But they become valuable for some other parties, say corporate companies and states, who make various assets out of it, such as profit, money, control, but most importantly, power.

So, there is a need to consider data as a right, just like our rights to life, liberty, livelihood or speech. The creator of data needs to own it. When appropriated, it turns against the creator itself. So, data rights of citizens are important and need to assert a strong claim at present. To bring our life under our control, we must at least now consider data as a product of our labour, so that it becomes our right.

# Endnotes

## Introduction

1. Miller, Claire Cain, and Nick Bilton, 'Google's Lab of Wildest Dreams', *The New York Times*, 13 November 2011, https://nyti.ms/3sFilr7. Accessed on 24 December 2021.
2. 'Most popular websites worldwide as of June 2021, by total visits', Statista, July 2021, https://bit.ly/33PtnQL. Accessed on 27 January 2022.
3. Grace, Katja, et al., 'Viewpoint: When will AI exceed human performance? Evidence from AI Experts', *Journal of Artificial Intelligence Research*, vol. 62, 2018, pp. 729–54, https://bit.ly/3FYcaS2. Accessed on 25 January 2022.
4. Boudry, Maarten, 'Human intelligence: have we reached the limit of knowledge?' *The Conversation*, 11 October 2019, https://bit.ly/3qWl2Dh. Accessed on 25 January 2022.
5. Litjens, Geert, et al., 'Clinical evaluation of a computer-aided diagnosis system for determining cancer aggressiveness in prostate MRI', *European Radiology*, vol. 25, no. 11, pp. 3187–99, https://bit.ly/3AAhfjr. Accessed on 22 November 2022.
6. Conger, Krista, 'Computers trounce pathologists in predicting lung cancer type, severity', *Stanford Medicine*, 16 August 2016, https://stan.md/3fRS7Ko. Accessed on 25 January 2022.

## Chapter 1

7. Oremus, Will, et al., 'How Facebook shapes your feed', *The Washington Post*, 26 October 2021, https://wapo.st/3KDXJGn. Accessed on 25 January 2022.
8. Cohen, David, 'Jack Dorsey Shed Some Light on How Twitter Uses Machine Learning, Deep Learning on Its Timeline', *Adweek*, 23 May 2017, https://bit.ly/3AsB0sa. Accessed on 25 January 2022.

9. IANS, 'Twitter uses deep learning to recommend tweets on timelines', *The Indian Express*, 10 May 2017, https://bit.ly/33OId9Z. Accessed on 25 January 2022.
10. Liu, Lijuan, Yanping Wang, and Wanle Chi, 'Image Recognition Technology Based on Machine Learning', *IEEE Access*, 4 September 2020, pp. 1-9, DOI: 10.1109/ACCESS.2020.3021590.
11. Crawford, Stephanie and Bernadette Johnson, 'How the Nest Learning Thermostat Works', How Stuff Works, 27 April 2021, https://bit.ly/3tXjgnB. Accessed on 25 January 2022.
12. Ong, Dominic, 'Yelp Restaurant Recommendation System—Data Science Capstone Project', *Towards Data Science*, 23 October 2020, https://bit.ly/3qYov4m. Accessed on 25 January 2022.
13. Sennaar, Kumba, 'Examples of AI in Restaurants and Food Services', Emerj, 31 January 2019, https://bit.ly/3Ir1QDM. Accessed on 25 January 2022.
14. Afprelaxnews, 'Artificial intelligence: Dating app users are increasingly trusting this matchmaker', *Forbes*, 27 July 2021, https://bit.ly/3458YXF. Accessed on 25 January 2022.

## Chapter 2

15. Matchar, Emily, 'Nine Tasks Robots Can Do That May Surprise You', *Smithsonian Magazine*, 5 September 2017, https://bit.ly/3HfbQzX. Accessed on 25 January 2022.
16. Southey, Flora, 'Online food delivery "one of the only winners" in coronavirus outbreak', Foodnavigator.com, 19 March 2020, https://bit.ly/3GYxDeQ. Accessed on 29 December 2021.
17. Dunbar, R.I.M., 'Breaking Bread: the Functions of Social Eating', *Adaptive Human Behavior and Physiology*, vol. 3, 11 March 2017, pp. 198–221, https://bit.ly/3IDtPjt. Accessed on 25 January 2022.
18. 'From Retailers to Insurance Providers, Here Are 21 Corps Using Drone Tech Today', *CBInsights*, 26 June 2019, https://bit.ly/3fWhmLG. Accessed on 25 January 2022.
19. Metz, Cade, 'How Driverless Cars See the World Around Them', *The New York Times*, 19 March 2018, https://nyti.ms/3FZsG40. Accessed on 25 January 2022.
20. Cusack, Jenny, 'How driverless cars will change our world', *BBC*,

30 November 2021, https://bbc.in/3H3icCm. Accessed on 25 January 2022.
21. Marr, Bernard, 'How Robots, IoT and Artificial Intelligence Are Changing How Humans Have Sex', *Forbes*, 1 April 2019, https://bit.ly/3nYlvmN. Accessed on 25 January 2022.
22. Prist, Anna, 'AI in a Sextech: the Future of Sex', Voice UI, 1 April 2020, https://bit.ly/32sxgtY. Accessed on 25 January 2022.
23. D'Sa, Francis, 'You should log out of Facebook before watching porn', *Deccan Chronicle*, 27 June 2016, https://bit.ly/3IDzcPF. Accessed on 25 January 2022.

## Chapter 3

24. Mayor, Adrienne, 'What Pandora's Box tells us about AI', World Economic Forum, 19 October 2018, https://bit.ly/3FWTtxV. Accessed on 25 January 2022.
25. Gerrish, Sean, *How Smart Machines Think*, MIT Press, 2018.
26. O'Connell, Sanjida, 'What the tortoise taught us', *The Guardian*, 7 December 2000, https://bit.ly/3FXoW3i. Accessed on 25 January 2022.
27. Haladjian, H.H., and Canlos Montemayor, 'Artificial consciousness and the consciousness-attention dissociation', *Consciousness and Cognition*, vol. 45, 2016, pp. 210–25, DOI: 10.1016/j.concog.2016.08.011.
28. Dilmegani, Cem, 'When will singularity happen? 995 experts' opinions on AGI', AI Multiple, 8 August 2017, https://bit.ly/3GYCvk8. Accessed on 25 January 2022.
29. Raj, Emmanuel, '8 Enablers For Europe's Trustworthy Artificial Intelligence', LinkedIn, 3 July 2019, https://bit.ly/3EPaGLe. Accessed on 29 November 2022.
30. Lycan, W.G., and Daniel Dennett, 'Consciousness Explained', *The Philosophical Review*, vol. 102, no. 3, July 1993, pp. 424–29, DOI: 10.2307/2185913. Accessed on 25 January 2022.
31. 'Kasparov vs. Deep Blue | The Match That Changed History', Chess.com, 12 October 2018, https://bit.ly/3rUjTf4. Accessed on 25 January 2022.
32. Silver, David, et al., 'Mastering the game of Go with deep neural networks and tree search', *Nature*, vol. 529, January 2016, pp. 484–89,

DOI: 10.1038/nature16961.

33   Bringsjord, Selmer, et al., 'Real robots that pass human tests of self-consciousness', 2015 24th IEEE International Symposium on Robot and Human Interactive Communication (RO-MAN), August 2015, pp. 498–504, DOI:10.1109/ROMAN.2015.7333698.

34   Shane, Scott, and Daisuke Wakabayashi, '"The Business of War": Google Employees Protest Work for the Pentagon', *The New York Times*, 4 April 2018, https://nyti.ms/35mJ7uQ. Accessed on 25 January 2022.

## Chapter 4

35   Moynihan, Qayyah, and Alba Asenjo, 'Facebook quietly ditched the "It's free and always will be" slogan from its homepage', *Insider*, 27 August 2019, https://bit.ly/3tYtXGw. Accessed on 25 January 2022.

36   Oremus, Will, 'Are You Really the Product?' *Slate*, 27 April 2018, https://bit.ly/3AtystL. Accessed on 25 January 2022.

37   Cellan-Jones, Rory, 'Stephen Hawking warns artificial intelligence could end mankind', BBC, 2 December 2014, https://bbc.in/3FWYmXN. Accessed on 1 January 2022.

38   Oremus, Will, 'Are You Really the Product?' *Slate*, 27 April 2018, https://bit.ly/3AtystL. Accessed on 25 January 2022.

39   James, William, *The Principles of Psychology: Volume 1*, Dover Publications, 1950.

40   Simon, Herbert A., et al., 'Designing Organizations for an Information-Rich World', *Computers, Communications, and the Public Interest*, 1971, pp. 37–52.

41   Ibid.

42   van Krieken, Robert, 'Georg Franck's "The Economy of Attention": Mental capitalism and the struggle for attention', *Journal of Sociology*, vol. 55, no. 1, 4 November 2018, pp. 3–7, DOI:10.1177/1440783318812111. Accessed on 29 December 2021.

43   Goldhaber, Michael H., 'The Attention Economy and the Net', *First Monday*, vol. 2, no. 4, 7 April 1997, https://bit.ly/3GP5LfQ.

44   Adityan, H., et al., 'Innovativeness and uniqueness as motivations for online shopping tendency and the mediating role of information

acquisition', *International Journal of Business Innovation and Research*, vol. 13, no. 1, 4 April 2017, pp. 30–51, https://bit.ly/3GGcPeH.

## Chapter 5

45  Schechner, Sam, and Mark Secada, 'You Give Apps Sensitive Personal Information. Then They Tell Facebook', *The Wall Street Journal*, 22 February 2019, https://on.wsj.com/3rRLTQt. Accessed on 25 January 2022.
46  Rivero, Nicolás, 'How to understand the extremely high stakes of Big Tech's antitrust battle', *Quartz*, 21 December 2020, https://bit.ly/3482d7q. Accessed on 25 January 2022.
47  Saran, Samir, 'Big Tech and the State: The necessity of regulating tech giants', Observer Research Foundation, 26 June 2021, https://bit.ly/3fWrUKM. Accessed on 25 January 2022.

## Chapter 6

48  Negroponte, Nicholas, *Being Digital*, Alfred A. Knopf, 1995.

## Chapter 7

49  Samuel, A.L., 'Some Studies in Machine Learning Using the Game of Checkers', *IBM Journal of Research and Development*, vol. 3, no. 3, July 1959, pp. 210–29. DOI:10.1147/rd.33.0210.
50  Grind, Kirsten, et al., 'How Google Interferes With Its Search Algorithms and Changes Your Results', *The Wall Street Journal*, 15 November 2019, https://on.wsj.com/3nY9SfE. Accessed on 25 January 2022.
51  Ofiwe, Michelle, 'How Does the Google Search Algorithm Work in 2021?' Semrush Blog, 8 October 2021, https://bit.ly/3Ax2sVO. Accessed on 25 January 2022.

## Chapter 8

52  Mascarenhas, Hyacinth, 'SXSW: Meet Sophia, the female humanoid robot that says she wants to start a family, destroy humans',

*International Business Times*, 21 March 2016, https://bit.ly/345bQno. Accessed on 25 January 2022.
53 Caballero, Maria Camila Gómez, 'The 5 most shocking phrases of Sophia, the AI robot that polarizes the world', *Impactotic*, 15 August 2018, https://bit.ly/3tXN8ju. Accessed on 25 January 2022.
54 Dearden, Lizzie, 'Japanese scientists create creepy robot newsreader with human face', *Independent*, 26 June 2014, https://bit.ly/3HfxKDb. Accessed on 25 January 2022.
55 Tangermann, Victor, 'Six Life-Like Robots That Prove The Future of Human Evolution is Synthetic', *Futurism*, 8 October 2017, https://bit.ly/3qX8efW. Accessed on 25 January 2022.
56 Stone, Zara, 'Everything You Need To Know About Sophia, The World's First Robot Citizen', *Forbes*, 7 November 2017, https://bit.ly/345tNSP. Accessed on 25 January 2022.

## Chapter 9

57 Adams, Tim, 'Self-driving cars: from 2020 you will become a permanent backseat driver', *The Guardian*, 13 September 2015, https://bit.ly/35bRoS8. Accessed on 25 January 2022.
58 Insider Intelligence, '10 million self-driving cars will be on the road by 2020', *Business Insider*, 15 June 2016, https://bit.ly/348mhpZ. Accessed on 25 January 2022.
59 Stewart, Emily, 'Self-driving cars have to be safer than regular cars. The question is how much', Vox, 17 May 2019, https://bit.ly/3fRjhRL. Accessed on 25 January 2022.
60 'Fatality Facts 2019: State by state', IIHS, March 2021, https://bit.ly/3tYHqOA. Accessed on 8 December 2022.
61 Lau, Andy, 'The Ethics of Self-Driving Cars', *Towards Data Science*, 5 March 2020. https://bit.ly/3r0qgOk. Accessed on 25 January 2022.
62 Alejandro, Edgard, 'Deontological Ethical System For Google's Self-Driving Car', California Polytechnic State University, Department of Computer Science, 31 May 2016, https://bit.ly/3nSI0JS. Accessed on 25 January 2022.
63 Chawla, Ayushmann, 'How Car Safety has Evolved Over Time – Know it More', News18, 21 May 2018, https://bit.ly/33PeptJ. Accessed on 25 January 2022.

64 Korosec, Kirsten, 'Ford postpones autonomous vehicle service until 2022', TechCrunch, 29 April 2020, https://tcrn.ch/3GVoQKG. Accessed on 25 January 2022.

65 Herrmann, Andreas, Brenner Walter and Rupert Stadler, *Autonomous Driving: How the Driverless Revolution Will Change the World*, Emerald Publishing Limited, 2018, p. 5.

66 Fingas, J., 'Audi's Grandsphere concept EV is a self-driving living room on wheels', Engadget, 2 September 2021, https://engt.co/33JtTzI. Accessed on 25 January 2022.

67 Bien, Calily, 'Self-driving supercar sets record at Circuit of the Americas', Kxan, 27 February 2017, https://bit.ly/3rQPVbt. Accessed on 25 January 2022.

68 Verheyde, Arne, 'NIO Autonomous Driving: Too Good To Be True', Seeking Alpha, 4 May 2021, https://bit.ly/3FSxatq. Accessed on 25 January 2022.

69 Ziegler, Chris, 'Riding in the Mercedes-Benz F 015', *The Verge*, 20 March 2015, https://bit.ly/3qXHT1p. Accessed on 25 January 2022.

70 Metz, Cade, and Neal E. Boudette, 'Inside Tesla as Elon Musk pushed an unflinching vision for self-driving cars', *The Economic Times*, 6 December 2021, https://bit.ly/3tX1dO5. Accessed on 25 January 2022.

71 Hawkins, Andrew J., 'Volvo confident it can get its "unsupervised" highway driving mode approved in California', *The Verge*, 5 January 2022, https://bit.ly/33PbKAn. Accessed on 25 January 2022.

72 '40+ Corporations Working On Autonomous Vehicles', *CB Insights*, 16 December 2020, https://bit.ly/3G47AS5. Accessed on 25 January 2022.

73 Herrmann, Andreas, Walter Brenner and Rupert Stadler, *Autonomous Driving: How the Driverless Revolution Will Change the World*, Emerald Publishing Limited, 2018, p. 9.

74 Ibid. 10.

## Chapter 10

75 Alferez, Alf, 'Top 10 Commercial Drone Delivery Companies', Ecommerce Next, 21 August 2021, https://bit.ly/3fUZXmI. Accessed on 25 January 2022.

76 Gallagher, Kevin, 'Drones: Public Safety Risk or Business Revolution?', Simulyze, 2 August 2016, https://bit.ly/3fWAY2k. Accessed on 25 January 2022.
77 'Dropped in for fruitless sex', Plant & Food Research, 4 April 2018, https://bit.ly/3KJ6rTO. Accessed on 25 January 2022.
78 Ashiq, Peerzada, 'LeT could be behind drone attack in Jammu, says DGP', *The Hindu*, 2 July 2021, https://bit.ly/32A1ziE. Accessed on 25 January 2022.

## Chapter 11

79 Ashton, K., 'That "Internet of Things" Thing', *RFiD Journal*, 22 June 2009, https://bit.ly/3EONmNB. Accessed on 29 November 2022.
80 'No Ordinary Disruption: The four forces breaking all the trends', McKinsey & Company, 13 April 2015, https://bit.ly/3FYyeMn. Accessed on 25 January 2022.
81 'Internet of Things (IoT) Market, 2021-2028', *Fortune Business Insights*, September 2021, https://bit.ly/3fX4y7C. Accessed on 25 January 2022.
82 'Internet of Things (IoT) Market – Growth, Trends, COVID-19 Impact, and Forecasts (2022–2027)', Mordor Intelligence, 2021, https://bit.ly/3EYmcVU. Accessed on 25 November 2022.
83 'Internet of Things (IoT) connected devices installed base worldwide from 2015 to 2025', Statista, 27 November 2016, https://bit.ly/3rLCFFf. Accessed on 25 January 2022.

## Chapter 12

84 Kowald, Dominik, and Elisabeth Lex, 'Studying Confirmation Bias in Hashtag Usage on Twitter', Graz University of Technology & Know-Center GmbH, 10 September 2018, https://bit.ly/3U9RMnY.
85 Pariser, Eli, *The Filter Bubble: What the Internet Is Hiding from You*, Penguin, 2011.
86 Bruns, A., 'Filter bubble', *Internet Policy Review*, vol. 8, no. 4, 29 November 2019, https://bit.ly/3ieEitN. Accessed on 8 December 2022.
87 Sunstein, Cass R., *Echo Chambers: Bush v. Gore, Impeachment, and Beyond*, Princeton University Press, 2001.

88  'Peter Wason', *The Telegraph*, 23 April 2003, https://bit.ly/3gL21Bu. Accessed on 29 November 2014.

## Chapter 13

89  Ambadi, 'Is Corruption an Issue in Indian Politics?' Thoughts, 16 October 2012, https://bit.ly/35sqq98. Accessed on 27 January 2022.
90  Pai, Nitin, 'FAQ: Why Anna Hazare is wrong and Lok Pal a bad idea', nitinpai.in, 14 August 2011, https://bit.ly/3GPJvTj. Accessed on 27 January 2022.
91  Ghosh, Avijit, '"Anna Hazare's movement is anti-social justice, manuwadi"', *The Times of India*, 19 August 2011, https://bit.ly/3u4DyeD. Accessed on 27 January 2022.
92  PR, Biju, 'Internet activism is a myth', Merinews, 31 December 2012, https://bit.ly/3o1lgHs. Accessed on 27 January 2022.
93  Hindman, Mathew, *The Myth of Digital Democracy*, Princeton University Press, 2008.
94  'Most Searched Female Celebrities of 2021: Kareena Kapoor Khan Leads, Katrina Kaif Takes 2nd Spot', *Outlook*, 4 December 2021, https://bit.ly/3r2HMSa. Accessed on 27 January 2022.
95  The term Web 2.0 was coined by Tim O'Reilly in 2005 as a common denominator for recent trends heading towards the ReadWrite Web. It allows everyone to publish resources on the web using simple and open, and personal and collaborative publishing tools, known as social software: blogs, wikis, social bookmarking systems, podcasts, etc. The main features of these tools are dynamism, openness and free availability. More accurately, in *Here Comes Everybody: The Power of Organizing Without Organizations* (2009), Clay Shirky discusses Web 2.0 as a coverlet phrase to portray new web applications such as Facebook, Twitter, Flickr, Blogger and YouTube that are user-centric and assist information sharing, collaboration and interactivity. It has been largely observed that Web 2.0 has altered communication from the familiar one-on-one, to one-to-many and many-to-many. For more details: O'Reilly, Tim, 'What Is Web 2.0: Design Patterns and Business Models for the Next Generation of Software', O'Reilly, 30 September 2005, https://bit.ly/34hgZJa. Accessed on 27 January 2022.

## Chapter 14

96 Froomkin, A. Michael, 'Big Data: Destroyer of Informed Consent', *Yale Journal of Health Policy, Law, and Ethics*, 23 June 2019, https://bit.ly/3r2M8Zt. Accessed on 27 January 2022.

## Chapter 15

97 Fuscaldo, Donna, 'Facebook Now Has More Users in India Than in Any Other Country', Investopedia, 25 June 2019, https://bit.ly/3fYIny7. Accessed on 27 January 2022.
98 Ahmed, Yasmin, 'WhatsApp may soon touch 500 million users in India despite new privacy policy, claims report', *Outlook*, 12 January 2021, https://bit.ly/34bQQes. Accessed on 27 January 2022.
99 'Leading countries based on Instagram audience size as of October 2021', Statista, October 2021, https://bit.ly/3u0TnmD. Accessed on 27 January 2022.
100 'Leading countries based on number of Twitter users as of October 2021', Statista, October 2021, https://bit.ly/3KPx9du. Accessed on 27 January 2022.
101 Dayalani, Vaishnavi, 'Flipkart, Amazon Or AJIO? India's Hottest Ecommerce Apps Of 2021', Inc42, 29 December 2021, https://bit.ly/3g33cs1. Accessed on 27 January 2022.
102 Madhok, Diksha, 'Uber partners with Meta to launch ride-booking via WhatsApp in India', CNN Business, 2 December 2021, https://cnn.it/33SBgVr. Accessed on 27 January 2022.
103 Taylor, Linnet, and Dennis Broeders, 'In the name of Development: Power, profit and the datafication of the global South', *Geoforum*, vol. 64, August 2015, pp. 229–37.
104 Glanz, James, and John Markoff, 'U.S. Underwrites Internet Detour Around Censors', *The NewYork Times*, 12 June 2011, https://nyti.ms/34bQ1T0. Accessed on 27 January 2022.
105 'Clinton: Internet "information curtain" is dropping', CNN, 21 January 2010, https://cnn.it/3fYOBxR. Accessed on 27 January 2022.
106 The term was used by the English-speaking Chinese newspaper *Global Times* in the context of privacy breach by Chinese Administration in the wake of Google allegation.

107 Bodeen, Christopher, 'China Slams Clinton's Internet Speech', *The San Diego Union Tribune*, 21 January 2010, https://bit.ly/33Y8Vgl. Accessed on 27 January 2022.
108 'Clinton: Internet "information curtain" is dropping', CNN, 21 January 2010, https://cnn.it/3fYOBxR. Accessed on 27 January 2022.
109 Srinivasan, Ramesh, and Adam Fish, 'Internet Authorship: Social and Political Implications Within Kyrgyzstan', *Journal of Computer-Mediated Communication*, 2009, https://bit.ly/3EDX1Xu. Accessed on 9 December 2022.
110 '10 Most Censored Countries', Committee to Protect Journalists, https://bit.ly/3rT3c3A. Accessed on 27 January 2022.
111 Dunne, Carey, 'Iran Arrests Eight Models for Posting "Un-Islamic" Photos on Instagram', HyperAllergic, 18 May 2016, https://bit.ly/35twyhm. Accessed on 27 January 2022.
112 Gos, Tricia, 'How to Do a Face Swap', Life Wire, 21 February 2021, https://bit.ly/3fXlxqF. Accessed on 27 January 2022.
113 Iyengar, Rishi, 'Twitter Caused a Furor by Suspending Parody Accounts of President Putin', *Time*, 2 June 2016, https://bit.ly/3g7NjR3. Accessed on 27 January 2022.
114 Bhaya, Abhishek G., 'Cambridge Analytica faces backlash in India, Kenya, Brazil, Mexico and Malaysia', CGTN, 23 March 2018, https://bit.ly/3H8RIPH. Accessed on 27 January 2022.
115 Advox, 'Can Facebook Connect the Next Billion?' Global Voices, 27 July 2017, https://bit.ly/3OIPDi2. Accessed on 29 November 2022.
116 Nyabola, Nanjala, 'Facebook's Free Basics Is an African Dictator's Dream', *Foreign Policy*, https://bit.ly/3u7il2z. Accessed on 29 November 2022.
117 Doctorow, Cory, '"Poor internet for poor people": India's activists fight Facebook connection plan', *The Guardian*, 15 January 2016, https://bit.ly/3o2rKG8. Accessed on 27 January 2022.
118 Kumar, Mohit, 'Facebook admits public data of its 2.2 billion users has been compromised', The Hacker News, 5 April 2018, https://bit.ly/33PCFw7. Accessed on 27 January 2022.
119 Punit, Itika Sharma, '335 Indians installed a Cambridge Analytica app, exposing the Facebook data of 560,000', *Quartz India*, 5 April 2018, https://bit.ly/3u8k3C3. Accessed on 27 January 2022.
120 Crabtree, Justina, 'Cambridge Analytica is an "example of what

modern day colonialism looks like," whistleblower says', CNBC, 27 March 2018, https://cnb.cx/35tzsCM. Accessed on 27 January 2022.
121 Crabtree, Justina, 'Here's how Cambridge Analytica played a dominant role in Kenya's chaotic 2017 elections', CNBC, 23 March 2018, https://cnb.cx/3H0q4Ex. Accessed on 27 January 2022.
122 'Did Cambridge Analytica use Filipinos' Facebook data to help Duterte win?' Rappler, YouTube, 5 April 2018, https://bit.ly/3u2e3cV. Accessed on 25 November 2022.
123 Houreld, Katharine, 'Foreigners working with Kenyan opposition manhandled by police before being deported', Reuters, 6 August 2017, https://reut.rs/3ACRVYQ. Accessed on 27 January 2022.
124 Choudhury, Angshuman, 'How Facebook Is Complicit in Myanmar's Attacks on Minorities', *The Diplomat*, 25 August 2020, https://bit.ly/3r4cDOf. Accessed on 27 January 2022.
125 Soteras, Eduardo, 'Social media misinformation stokes a worsening civil war in Ethiopia', NPR, 15 October 2021, https://n.pr/3u3yE1v. Accessed on 27 January 2022.
126 'Report of the National Hearing on Racism and Social Media in South Africa: 15–16 February 2017', South African Human Rights Commission, August 2017, https://bit.ly/3H8kxM7. Accessed on 27 January 2022.
127 Benedictus, Leo, 'Invasion of the troll armies: from Russian Trump supporters to Turkish state stooges', *The Guardian*, 6 November 2016, https://bit.ly/3s1dONY. Accessed on 27 January 2022.
128 'China's Internet Trolls Go Global', Council on Foreign Affairs, 7 June 2021, https://on.cfr.org/3ABI45M. Accessed on 27 January 2022.
129 Jones, Katie, 'Ranked: The World's Most Downloaded Apps', Visual Capitalist, 25 January 2020, https://bit.ly/3IEi0d5. Accessed on 27 January 2022.

## Chapter 16

130 Timberg, Craig, and Tony Romm, 'The U.S. government fined the app now known as TikTok $5.7 million for illegally collecting children's data', *The Washington Post*, 27 February 2019, https://wapo.st/3H0sVNL. Accessed on 27 January 2022.
131 Meyer, David, 'Twitter Under Formal Investigation for How It

Tracks Users in the GDPR Era', *Fortune*, 12 October 2018, https://bit.ly/3rUyJ51. Accessed on 27 January 2022.

132 Rosemain, Mathieu, 'France fines Google $57 million for European privacy rule breach', Reuters, 22 January 2019, https://reut.rs/3IDRT5W. Accessed on 27 January 2022.

133 Arthur, Charles, 'Google "faces $22.5m fine over Safari privacy breach"', *The Guardian*, 11 July 2012, https://bit.ly/3KR7Asj. Accessed on 27 January 2022.

134 Koeneman, Briana, 'YouTube Accused of Illegally Collecting Data from Children', Newsy, 9 April 2018, https://bit.ly/3KNTEPR. Accessed on 27 January 2022.

135 Kantaria, Priya, 'Amazon data leaks: Has the ecommerce giant fallen foul of GDPR?', Verdict, 17 September 2018, https://bit.ly/3o2qH9k. Accessed on 27 January 2022.

136 Boland, Hanna, 'Amazon data breach reveals private details of customers ahead of Black Friday', *The Telegraph*, 21 November 2018, https://bit.ly/3g1eqgN. Accessed on 27 January 2022.

137 'Uber Gets Hefty Fine from the EU for Data Breach', Connectech, 12 December 2018, https://bit.ly/3AEJzQz. Accessed on 27 January 2022.

138 Marr, Bernard, 'GDPR: The Biggest Data Breaches and the Shocking Fines (That Would Have Been)', *Forbes*, 11 June 2018, https://bit.ly/3G3R2de. Accessed on 27 January 2022.

139 Ghoshal, Devjyot, 'Mapped: The breathtaking global reach of Cambridge Analytica's parent company', *Quartz*, 29 March 2018, https://bit.ly/3KJiX5P. Accessed on 27 January 2022.

140 'Cambridge Analytica: The data firm's global influence', BBC News, 22 March 2018, https://bbc.in/35sCqYe. Accessed on 27 January 2022.

141 Lecher, Colin, 'Former Cambridge Analytica employee says Facebook users affected could be "much greater than 87 million"', *The Verge*, 17 April 2018, https://bit.ly/3u9LxHH. Accessed on 27 January 2022.

142 Chan, Rosalie, 'The Cambridge Analytica whistleblower explains how the firm used Facebook data to sway elections', *Business Insider,* 6 October 2019, https://bit.ly/3H6glN7. Accessed on 27 January 2022.

143 Ingram, David, 'Facebook says data leak hits 87 million users, widening privacy scandal', Reuters, 4 April 2018, https://reut.

rs/3rRD3C1. Accessed on 27 January 2022.
144 Bhattacharya, Devika, 'Whistleblower says Cambridge Analytica "worked extensively" in India, names Congress as client', *The Times of India*, 27 March 2018, https://bit.ly/3r4AOfF. Accessed on 27 January 2022.
145 Sinha, Smita, 'Cambridge Analytica Whistleblower Christopher Wylie Says Congress Was A Client', *Analytics India Magazine*, 28 March 2018, https://bit.ly/3H1A14y. Accessed on 27 January 2022.
146 'Congress, BJP in Twitter war over NaMo app', *The Hindu*, 25 March 2018, https://bit.ly/3KMGDWG. Accessed on 27 January 2022.
147 'NaMo app controversy: US-based firm says it doesn't sell or rent data', *Hindustan Times*, 27 March 2018, https://bit.ly/3ACBThR. Accessed on 27 January 2022.
148 Venugopal, Vasudha, 'Elliot Alderson may be a French network and telecommunications engineer', *The Economic Times*, 27 March 2018, https://bit.ly/3FZmCZD. Accessed on 27 January 2022.
149 'BJP, Congress apps in data privacy row: All you need to know about the debate', *Hindustan Times*, 27 March 2018, https://bit.ly/33ZQGqO. Accessed on 27 January 2022.
150 'An IIT graduate has been arrested for illegally accessing the Aadhaar database: Report', *Firstpost*, 4 August 2017, https://bit.ly/3g6vvWs. Accessed on 27 January 2022.
151 Khaira, Rachna, 'Rs 500, 10 minutes, and you have access to billion Aadhaar details', *The Tribune*, 5 January 2018, https://bit.ly/33NxDjH. Accessed on 27 January 2022.
152 Kodali, Srinivas, 'UIDAI's Defensive Stance on Aadhaar Security Breaches Isn't Helping Anybody but the Government', *The Wire*, 5 January 2018, https://bit.ly/3o23fsI. Accessed on 27 January 2022.

## Chapter 17

153 For three recent introductions to surveillance literature, see Lyon, David *Surveillance Studies*, Polity, 2007; Haggerty, Kevin D., and Minas Samatas (eds), *Surveillance and Democracy*, Routledge-Cavendish, 2010; and Hier, Sean P., and Joshua Greenberg (eds), *The Surveillance Studies Reader*, Open University Press, 2007.
154 For example, Progressive Insurance's 'My Rate' programme offers

reduced insurance rates in exchange of installation of a device that monitors driving speed, time and habits; Peppet, Scott R., 'Unraveling Privacy: The Personal Prospectus and the Threat of a Full-Disclosure Future', *Northwestern University Law Review*, 2011, p. 1153, p. 1156.

155 Sottek, T.C., and Janus Kopfstein, 'Everything you need to know about PRISM', *The Verge*, 17 July 2013, https://bit.ly/3487onM. Accessed on 27 January 2022.

156 Mezzofiore, Gianluca, 'NSA Whistleblower Edward Snowden: Washington Snoopers Are Criminals', *International Business Times*, 17 June 2013, https://bit.ly/3g4pkCx. Accessed on 27 January 2022.

157 Seifert, Dan, 'Secret program gives NSA, FBI backdoor access to Apple, Google, Facebook, Microsoft data', *The Verge*, 6 June 2013, https://bit.ly/3ABNYDY. Accessed on 27 January 2022.

158 'EU-USA: Data Surveillance: The Washington Post publishes new documents on PRISM', Statewatch, 1 July 2013, https://bit.ly/3fXwhoZ. Accessed on 27 January 2022.

159 'ITU releases latest tech figures & global rankings', Satellite Markets & Research, https://bit.ly/3HLNfFF. Accessed on 19 December 2022.

160 Rich, Steven, and Barton Gellman, 'NSA seeks to build quantum computer that could crack most types of encryption', *The Washington Post*, 2 January 2014, https://wapo.st/3H5ZytB. Accessed on 27 January 2022.

161 'Utah Data Center', Domestic Surveillance Directorate, https://bit.ly/3r3CfL6. Accessed on 27 January 2022.

162 Boon, Floor, Steven Derix and Huib Modderkolk, 'NSA infected 50,000 computer networks with malicious software', NRC, https://bit.ly/3H6eE1X. Accessed on 27 January 2022.

163 McCoy, Alfred, 'Surveillance and scandal: time-tested weapons for US global power', Open Democracy, 20 January 2014, https://bit.ly/3H6F57T. Accessed on 27 January 2022.

164 *Communications Surveillance in India*, SFLC.in, 2014, https://bit.ly/3FFf6ER. Accessed on 19 December 2022.

165 Singh, Shalini, 'India's surveillance project may be as lethal as PRISM', *The Hindu*, 21 June 2013, https://bit.ly/3rUXj5R. Accessed on 27 January 2022.

166 Tiwari, Udbhav, 'The Design & Technology behind India's Surveillance Programmes', The Centre for Internet and Society, 20 January 2017,

https://bit.ly/3g1Yafw. Accessed on 27 January 2022.
167 Satish, Mrinal, '"Bad Characters, History Sheeters, Budding Goondas and Rowdies": Police Surveillance Files and Intelligence Databases in India', *National Law School of India Review*, vol. 23, no. 1, 6 November 2010, p. 133, https://bit.ly/34eKsTJ. Accessed on 27 January 2022.
168 Xynou, Maria, 'Big democracy, big surveillance: India's surveillance state', Open Democracy, 10 February 2014, https://bit.ly/3s1tYa6. Accessed on 27 January 2022.
169 Khaira, Rachna, 'Rs 500, 10 minutes, and you have access to billion Aadhaar details', *The Tribune*, 3 January 2018, https://bit.ly/3UgVtbH. Accessed on 27 January 2022.
170 Marx, Gary T., 'Seeing Hazily, But Not Darkly, Through the Lens: Some Recent Empirical Studies of Surveillance Technologies', *Law and Social Inquiry*, vol. 30, no. 2, 2005, https://bit.ly/3g1KAc3. Accessed on 27 January 2022.
171 Xynou, Maria, 'Interview with Caspar Bowden—Privacy Advocate and former Chief Privacy Adviser at Microsoft', The Centre for Internet and Society, 6 November 2013, https://bit.ly/3r10lGu. Accessed on 27 January 2022.
172 'Keynote—Jacob Appelbaum', Linux.conf.au 2012, Ballarat, Australia, YouTube, 21 January 2012, https://bit.ly/3AzAl8a. Accessed on 27 January 2022.

## Chapter 18

173 Salge, Carolina, and Nicholas Berente, 'Is That Social Bot Behaving Unethically?' *Communications of the ACM*, vol. 60, no. 9, September 2017, pp. 29–31.
174 Wu, F., et al., 'A New Approach to Bot Detection: Striking the Balance between Precision and Recall', 2016 IEEE/ACM International Conference on Advances in Social Networks Analysis and Mining (ASONAM), 2016, pp. 533–40, https://bit.ly/3gyD78n.
175 Vosoughi, S., D. Roy and S. Aral, 'The Spread of True and False News Online', *Science*, vol. 359, no. 6380, March 2018, pp. 1146–51, https://bit.ly/2RCcUTX.
176 Nield, David, 'You Probably Don't Know All the Ways Facebook

Tracks You', Gizmodo, 8 June 2017, https://bit.ly/3nXWloj. Accessed on 27 January 2022.
177 'How Tech Companies Track Your Every Move and Put Your Data Up for Sale', NPR, 31 July 2019, https://n.pr/3u53oPR. Accessed on 27 January 2022.
178 Albright, John, '#Election2016: Propaganda-lytics & Weaponized Shadow Trackers', Medium, 22 November 2016, https://bit.ly/3r4jFTe. Accessed on 27 January 2022.

## Chapter 19

179 Samim, 'Assisted Writing Reimagining Word Processing', Medium, 7 June 2017, https://bit.ly/3fZ8mFF. Accessed on 27 January 2022.

## Chapter 20

180 'Alphabet's Next Billion-Dollar Business: 12 Industries To Watch', *CB Insight*, 1 June 2021, https://bit.ly/3H8EW3F. Accessed on 27 January 2022.
181 Hobbes, Thomas, *Leviathan*, Penguin Books, 1968.
182 Brynjolfsson, Erik, and Andrew McAfee, *The Second Machine Age: Work, Progress, and Prosperity in a Time of Brilliant Technologies*, W.W. Norton & Company, 2016.

# Acknowledgements

To Gayu, my wife and soulmate, the best-ever person by my side—for her expert opinion, patience, tolerance and incredible heart. She always tells me what I write isn't perfect. I revised what I typed to get her appreciation. So far, I didn't get it. Thanks for never telling me what I wanted to hear from you. But I listened a million times, silently you telling me what I wanted to hear. Machines cannot visualize like this.

Ashima, Ameya and Ashiq—the cutest and smallest; machines will be boring after a while. Your Valyapapa is waiting to see that you are growing as humans—knowing, listening, learning, loving, waiting, caring...

Acha and Ammachi, I am what I am today because of you two.

For Shiju, my brother. I owe you a great debt.

Parvathy, Nandhu, Devan, Abhi and Thumbi, your generation will never read books unless someone reminds you. As we know it today, books will not remain so when you become adults. I still hope about your generation. Machines never hope like humans.

Nadha Noureen C.K., machines never get bored, but humans will. Only love makes you read the earlier drafts two times. Even though machines reportedly write books and articles, they never love what they do. Thank you for your intervention.

Jagannathan Gopinathan, AI researcher, Cognizant Technology. Thanks for calling me one Friday evening and talking to me for more than one hour about AI. I owe you an enormous debt of gratitude. Still, machines cannot express gratitude.

For Yamini Chowdhury, the best commissioning editor I met.

She was very much helping and quick to respond to my emails at Rupa. Thank you for giving me this opportunity.

For Aurodeep Mukherjee and Vicky Sharma, the promising editors at Rupa patiently worked on copy editing and corrected many issues with the manuscript. Thank you for the eye for detail.

Everyone who helped me, directly and indirectly, create this book, thank you all.